Frank

PREHISTORIC DARTMOOR

PREHISTORIC DARTMOOR

By PAUL PETTIT

(With an Introduction by Tom Greeves, M.A., Ph.D.)

FOREST PUBLISHING

First published 1974

Re-published, with a new Introduction by Tom Greeves, B.A., Ph.D., in 1995 by FOREST PUBLISHING, Woodstock, Liverton, Newton Abbot, Devon TQ12 6JJ

British Library Cataloguing in Publication Data

A catalogue record for this book is available from the British Library.

ISBN 0-9515274-6-0

Forest Publishing

Editorial, design and colour photography by:
Mike Lang

Typeset by:
Carnaby Typesetting, Torquay, Devon TQ1 1EG

Printed and bound in Great Britain by:
BPC Wheatons Ltd., Exeter, Devon EX2 8RP

CONTENTS

LIST OF ILLUSTRATIONS

PLATES

IN TEXT

INTRODUCTION

A Dartmoor without reaves, without radiocarbon dates for prehistory and without a Sites and Monuments Register listing all known archaeological features of the moor seems almost inconceivable to us now. Yet when Paul Pettit's book was first published in 1974, this was more or less the situation regarding Dartmoor prehistory. Moreover, for nearly twenty years his book remained the only serious attempt to present all known information about prehistoric Dartmoor in a popular format.

In the preceding twenty years, since the publication of R. Hansford Worth's *Dartmoor* (edited by Spooner and Russell in 1953) notable excavations had taken place at Dean Moor and at Kestor, which Pettit describes, but otherwise the state of archaeological knowledge had not substantially advanced since the time of the Dartmoor Exploration Committee who began excavating at Grimspound in 1894. *Prehistoric Dartmoor* remains a comprehensive and very accessible summary of the work of these pioneers, with useful accounts of Lady Aileen Fox's excavations of the 1950s. The book contains fine photographs of both sites and artefacts, plus sketch maps to guide the reader.

Pettit includes some good insights, such as comparing prehistoric sites with decaying churches of the present day (p.33), commenting on prehistoric notions of privacy (pp. 42 and 44), noting the false-crest positioning of many cairns, and arguing for their constructional sophistication — 'not just heaps of earth and stone' (p.92).

He described a few newly recorded sites such as the 'Sowton' (i.e. Sourton) stone circle (p.138) which had been obscurely

1

reported in the *Devon Archaeological Exploration Society Newsletter* No. 15 (1966) pp. 5–6, but in most instances he used only the major runs of academic journals as his source. This means that some other sites, which had not been long known by the early 1970s, such as the stone circle on Mardon Down, the triple stone row on Holne Moor, the row on Walkhampton Common above Horseyeatt, and the row crossing the watershed of Piles Hill, do not receive a mention. Most of these 'new' sites are now marked on Ordnance Survey maps, as are countless others discovered in the last twenty years. For example, Pettit noted some 300 cairns (p.91), but now more than 1000 have been recorded.

Archaeology is a very dynamic discipline, with new material constantly being recorded, some of which can radically alter established theories. The two decades since Pettit's book first appeared have seen a remarkable accumulation of information about the prehistory of Dartmoor, though our understanding and interpretation of it remains largely in the sphere of intelligent guesswork.

Prehistoric Dartmoor could hardly have appeared at a more significant time as far as the study of Dartmoor's prehistory is concerned. Although the 1960s had seen relatively little progress, exciting developments in archaeological awareness were stirring at the end of that decade, especially regarding the now familiar 'reaves' or land boundaries. Pettit did not mention the word 'reave' in his book and, like most of his contemporaries (whether academics or not), missed the significance of a paper published in 1968 in Volume 100 of the *Transactions of the Devonshire Association*, titled 'Parallel Reaves on Dartmoor' by Elizabeth Gawne and John Somers Cocks. Pettit, following others, was content to refer to what we now know as prehistoric parallel reaves as post-prehistoric 'long strips' (p.80) or 'medieval strips' (p.85).

In fact, the paper by Gawne and Somers Cocks was the start of a reassessment of these boundaries and of recognition of their prehistoric date. At much the same time that Pettit's book appeared an article was published in the *Proceedings of the Devon Archaeological Society* (1973) by Andrew Fleming and others on 'A late Prehistoric Reave System near Cholwich Town, Dartmoor'. This was the first report on what became a major fieldwork project, culminating in the publication of Andrew Fleming's own book *The Dartmoor Reaves: Investigating Prehistoric Land Divisions* (Batsford, 1988). In landscape terms the work of Andrew Fleming has revolutionised our understanding of the coherence of prehistoric Dartmoor in the second millennium BC, by demonstrating a land marked out by territorial boundaries (reaves) sometimes many kilometres in length, and also by complex 'co-axial' field systems (parallel reaves).

Detailed field survey since Pettit was writing has filled many gaps in our knowledge of the distribution of sites. Tribute must be paid to L. V. Grinsell who published a remarkable corpus on barrows in 1978 (see Select Bibliography). This was complemented by a paper by J. Turner, published in 1990, on ring cairns and related features which seem to form an essential element of Dartmoor prehistoric funerary structures. But for overall plotting and record of the prehistoric landscape of Dartmoor pride of place must go to Jeremy Butler whose publication of a four-volume *Dartmoor Atlas of Antiquities* was completed in 1994.

We now have several radiocarbon dates from Dartmoor — from reaves at Saddlesborough and on Holne Moor, and from settlement sites on Shaugh Moor and at Gold Park. These provide the material for the first cautious attempts at an absolute chronology of Dartmoor prehistory. A useful chart of prehistoric radiocarbon dates from Devon as a whole was published in 1988 by Henrietta Quinnell (see Select Bibliography). This reminds us that Dartmoor should not be considered in isolation.

The earliest phase of the reaves, when they consisted of ditches and banks with or without fences, can be placed before 1500 BC. In broad terms the great stone reave-building phase on Dartmoor would seem to fit securely within the mid-second millennium BC. The settlement at Shaugh Moor, which was fully excavated, may have been occupied for some one thousand years, from the early second to the early first millennium BC. In its early phases the five huts were unenclosed. In contrast, the settlement at Gold Park, excavated by Alex Gibson in the 1980s, fits firmly within the late prehistoric period, its early timber phase belonging to the 4th/3rd century BC and later stone phase to the 2nd/1st century BC.

Each of these modern excavations has demonstrated unequivocally that timber was a major component of prehistoric structures on Dartmoor. On both Holne Moor and Shaugh Moor evidence of timber buildings was found, dating to the 2nd millennium BC and either pre-dating or being contemporary with stone structures. On both Holne Moor and at Saddlesborough, timber was found to be associated with early reaves, as fencing. More surprisingly, perhaps, was the discovery of late prehistoric timber buildings at Gold Park, suggesting that throughout prehistory wooden structures may have coexisted with stone ones on Dartmoor. Indeed, such practice is most unlikely to have been limited to boundaries and huts, and recently it has been suggested by Henrietta Quinnell that the Cholwich Town stone row (described by Pettit, pp. 137–8) may have had an early timber phase.

Pettit gives good coverage of the prehistoric pots known as beakers which, on Dartmoor, have been found exclusively associated with cists (Pettit uses an old-fashioned 'kist' spelling). No longer can we link beakers with any particular invasive group of 'Beaker people' (Pettit, p.22), and the Dartmoor examples can-

4

not be confidently separated chronologically, though the one from Langcombe (Pettit, p.122) may be 'early', i.e. late 3rd millennium BC, while the others broadly fit within the first few centuries of the 2nd millennium BC.

Archaeology remains one of the most rapidly developing disciplines. New data and new ideas are constantly being assimilated. Period divisions such as 'Neolithic', 'Bronze Age' and 'Iron Age' are seen to be too simplistic to adequately reflect the complexity of prehistoric life, and many archaeologists prefer to speak of particular millennia where possible. What were seemingly cosy and secure theories can suddenly become much more exposed — for example, the defended hilltops on the fringes of Dartmoor used all to be placed within the first millennium BC. Many still belong there, but White Tor, for instance (Pettit, p.179) is now thought possibly to date to the third or even fourth millennium BC and may have had a function as an enclosure around sacred cairns (inf. H. Quinnell). Even the much vaunted 'climatic deterioration' of the first millennium BC is open to question, there being no environmental evidence from Dartmoor to support it, as yet (inf. C. Caseldine).

Pettit's book should not be used as a textbook, but should be seen as an accurate statement of ideas about the prehistory of Dartmoor as they had developed from the 1890s until about the mid-1960s. His main and lasting achievement was to set out clearly in print a summary of known archaeological work carried out over this seventy year period, the detailed reports of which were only available in academic journals. However, it is interesting to note that Pettit obviously felt moved by the experience of seeing so much evidence of remote human activity on the open moorland. He wrote (p.34), 'A wanderer across the uplands and the deep valleys is made vividly aware of the early Moormen'. The text of his book ends (p.182) with an imaginary scenario of ponies on Dartmoor in 'the last two centuries BC'. How pleased he must have been to learn that hoofprints of ponies were found in a ditch of a reave under excavation in 1980 on Saddlesborough, and that they were dated some fifteen hundred years earlier to the mid-2nd millennium BC — the very period which features so largely in his book, and which he had so successfully brought within the grasp of an interested general readership!

NOTE: Pettit's book is mostly accurately typeset, the only significant misspelling that readers will notice is 'millenium' and 'millenia'. The placename 'Whittenknowles Rocks' is misspelt (p.78) and the site wrongly described as an open settlement when it is actually enclosed.
Pettit uses imperial measurements throughout the book. To convert feet to metres multiply by 0.305. To convert inches to millimetres multiply by 25.4.

SELECT BIBLIOGRAPHY
(of publications on Dartmoor prehistory since 1974)

NOTE: all known Dartmoor publications are now listed in *The Dartmoor Bibliography* (Devon Books, 1992) by Peter Hamilton-Leggett. The book has a comprehensive index. Supplements 1 and 2 were published in 1993 and 1994 respectively.

<u>General</u>
Butler, Jeremy (1991–4) *Dartmoor Atlas of Antiquities*, Volumes 1–4 (Devon Books, Exeter) — a comprehensive mapping of all archaeological features on the moor (Volume 5 is scheduled for publication in 1995).

Reaves

Fleming, Andrew (1978) 'The Prehistoric Landscape of Dartmoor. Part 1: South Dartmoor', *Proc. Prehistoric Society*, 44, 97–123

Fleming, Andrew (1983) 'The Prehistoric Landscape of Dartmoor, Part 2: North and East Dartmoor', *Proc. Prehistoric Society*, 49, 195–241

Fleming, Andrew (1988) *The Dartmoor Reaves: Investigating Prehistoric Land Divisions* (Batsford, London)

Shaugh Moor and Saddlesborough Excavations

Wainwright, G. J., Fleming, A. and Smith, K. (1979) 'The Shaugh Moor Project: First Report', *Proc. Prehistoric Society*, 45, 1–35

Wainwright, G. J. and Smith, K. (1980) 'The Shaugh Moor Project: Second Report — the enclosures', *Proc. Prehistoric Society*, 46, 65–122

Smith, K., Coppen, J., Wainwright, G. J. and Beckett, S. (1981) 'The Shaugh Moor Project: Third Report — Settlement and Environmental Investigations', *Proc. Prehistoric Society*, 47, 205–273

Balaam, N. D., Smith, K. and Wainwright, G. J. (1982) 'The Shaugh Moor Project: Fourth Report — Environment, Context and Conclusion', *Proc. Prehistoric Society*, 48, 203–278

Gold Park (North Bovey) Excavations

Gibson, Alex (1992) 'The Excavation of an Iron Age Settlement at Gold Park, Dartmoor', *Proc. Devon Archaeological Society*, 50, 19–46

Barrows

Turner, J. R. (1980) 'Chamber Cairns, Gidleigh', *Proc. Devon Archaeological Society*, 38, 117–119

Grinsell, L. V. (1978) 'Dartmoor Barrows', *Proc. Devon Archaeological Society*, 36, 85–180

Turner, J. R. (1990) 'Ring Cairns, Stone Circles and Related Monuments on Dartmoor', *Proc. Devon Archaeological Society*, 48, 27–86

Chronology

Quinnell, H (1988) 'The Local Character of the Devon Bronze Age and its Interpretation in the 1980s', *Proc. Devon Archaeological Society*, 46, 1–12

Most prehistoric sites are marked on the Ordnance Survey map *Outdoor Leisure 28* which is at a scale of 1:25000 (2¹/₂ inches to the mile), and which covers the whole of Dartmoor.

The *Sites and Monuments Register* is a county-wide archive of archaeology, at County Hall, Topsham Road, Exeter. It can be consulted by appointment.

★★★★★

Tom Greeves, M.A., Ph. D.
Tavistock
January 1995

FOREWORD

Many relics of prehistoric man lie scattered about Dartmoor's open, rolling hills and enchanting valleys, and the remains of over two thousand buildings and of several hundred tombs can be recognised. With the passing of time the ruined settlements and monuments have become an integral part of the landscape, adding an element of mystery to the natural beauty. Even the casual visitor is prompted to inquire about the significance of the relics, and why the inhospitable Moor was so attractive to prehistoric man?

Quite a lot has already been written about the prehistoric Moor, as the Bibliography at the end of this book shows. But the literature consists entirely of articles dealing with particular aspects, summaries or references in books of wider scope, and reports in the *Transactions of the Devonshire Association*. Little of this is available to the visitors who come to the Moor in increasing numbers each year.

One reason for the lack of a book devoted solely to the prehistory of the Moor may be that many aspects are still obscure—as obscure as the Moor itself when clouds cover it. In spite of excavations and surveys since World War II, in spite of soil pollen analyses that have made the picture of the physical environment clearer, many problems remain unsolved and much work needs to be done. The most difficult problem is the time sequence, which is still not clear in detail. No absolute dates are available on which to base a story, and carbon-dating technique has not yet been applied to samples from Dartmoor.

9

Nevertheless, a general account—a review of past explorations, a record of the most important relics, a summary of present knowledge—is overdue.

The area covered by this book is the high plateau known as the Forest of Dartmoor and its surrounding Commons. Except for parts of the south-western border, it is over 1,000ft above sea level, and bounded by escarpments plunging down to a different environment. The National Park boundary has been drawn wider, to include outlying granite masses and large belts of the border country, but in a prehistoric context the great plateau is a convenient entity. Reference will only be made to the border country where relevant.

Map squares or six-figure map references are given for those sites which are not marked on, or are not easy to identify from, the one-inch Ordnance Survey sheets.

Many people have helped with the preparation of this book. My special thanks go to Miss S. M. Pearce (Museum Curator of Antiquities, Exeter City) for much information and advice, also to Mr James Barber (Assistant Curator, Plymouth City Museum) for his ready co-operation. I am grateful to Mr C. A. Lilley for photographs, to Mr James Pettit for photographs and plans, and to Miss P. F. Humphries for invaluable help with correspondence. Mr Gordon Winter has kindly given permission for the use of his translation of an extract from Caesar's *Gallic War*.

Figs 6, 10, 13 and 14b are based on the Ordnance Survey maps with the sanction of the Controller of Her Majesty's Stationery Office, Crown Copyright reserved.

Figs 5, 7, 8, 11 and 12 are based on plans and drawings which first appeared in the *Transactions of the Devonshire Association*.

I

THE PRIMEVAL WASTE

Ten thousand years ago Dartmoor was almost certainly a wilderness untrodden by man. During the hundreds of milleniums conveniently labelled the Palaeolithic or Old Stone Age, the first Devonians—a mere handful of men—left no evidence that they used it. They lived in caves near what was to become the south coast of Devon and were hunters, fishers and food-gatherers who could satisfy their needs without climbing the steep valleys which surrounded the highlands. For long periods during the Old Stone Age the Moor, though not glaciated, offered a bleak, cold environment. Man could have hunted there during the warmer, interglacial periods, but up to forty years ago no Palaeolithic find had been recorded.

One day in May 1931 R. Hansford Worth, a great explorer of Dartmoor and an indefatigable recorder of its antiquities, made a dramatic find. This was a flint hand-axe, a little over four inches in length, which he picked up on Brent Moor and which he recognised to be of Palaeolithic type. 'Its appearance,' he reported modestly, 'is consistent with, but does not fully imply, a great age ... The one certainty is that it adds to the published record of Dartmoor a new form of implement; which may be a relic of palaeolithic man ...'

The axe, an all-purpose tool, has been dated by comparison

11

with examples found elsewhere to 170,000/110,000 BC. This was the third interglacial era when the Moor could have been accessible to man. But since the find remains unique, and the tool could have been dropped by a later wanderer, it cannot by itself be accepted as proof of man's presence in Palaeolithic times.

As recently as ten thousand years ago the Moor may therefore reasonably be pictured as an untrodden waste—a rugged fist of granite pushed up through the sedimentary rocks in some ancient upheavals. It was a valley-scarred plateau with an area of something over two hundred square miles. The scenery was open heathland, the soil decomposed granite, and the blanket bog had not yet formed. Many of the sombre hills rose, as now, to fantastic rock piles, and their slopes were strewn with clatters of granite boulders. In the valleys, the streams and rivers rushed in their rocky beds among hazel scrub and clumps of pine and birch. No animal bones have survived in the acid soil to show that deer, wolf, bear, wild cattle and pig roamed over the upland. It is likely that these, and many smaller animals like the fox and badger, and many birds, lived in the valleys and on the hills. All these would one day supply man with food or clothing, or perhaps prey on his flocks. Meanwhile, through interminable centuries, the seasons revolved over a wilderness. The landscape reflected the changing moods of the sky, one day beautiful beyond description, the next cloud-wrapped and forbidding. The physical contrast of waste and beauty, of windswept uplands and sheltered valleys, was waiting to tantalise and repel man.

MESOLITHIC WANDERERS

About 8000 BC man began to penetrate the Moor. Mesolithic or Middle Stone Age culture had for some millenia replaced

FIG. 1.
PRE-BRONZE AGE
SITES

the Palaeolithic. The men were still small groups of hunters and food-gatherers but, owing to the improving climate, no longer based on caves. They are shadowy figures because their dead have not been found in Britain.

Mesolithic culture was characterised by very small weapons and tools—some no larger than a thumb nail—called microliths. The primary purpose was hunting, the implements mostly scrapers of flint or chert cores, and tiny flint blades flaked from cores and fixed on wooden shafts to make arrows and spears. With these light weapons Mesolithic man spread all over southern Britain, leaving scatterings of their weapons from Kent to Land's End.

Flint and chert are not natural to the Moor and were imported. Microliths have been found at Taw Marsh in the north and in half a dozen localities on the eastern fringes (Fig 1). Over eighteen hundred worked flints were collected on Gidleigh Common and several thousand at Batworthy on the opposite side of the North Teign river. At Fernworthy some arrowheads and hundreds of discarded scraps were evidence of Mesolithic flint-working near the site of the modern reservoir. From Holwell Tor came an unusually fine blade, 3in long and trimmed down both edges. A granite pounding stone of Mesolithic type was found in a field at Welstor, north-east of Ashburton, along with flint flakes.

Deeper penetration of the Moor is evidenced by discoveries of microliths at Runnage and Ringhill (647794), both near Postbridge. At the latter, a large number of microliths, cores, and micro-burins (the rejected pieces of core after a microlith had been detached) were found buried under a foot of peat.

The Mesolithic people were nomads and the sites where they have left traces of their passing are usually near springs. These places seem to have been camps rather than permanent settlements. It is probable that in suitable areas they wandered

14

in a yearly cycle, and Dartmoor would have been one such area.

Twenty years ago some Mesolithic sites at Week (sq 6692), a mile off the plateau in the north-east foothills, were investigated. They were near springs, on south-facing slopes, at a height of 850–900ft above sea level, and they produced many microliths and thousands of flint scraps, cores, and partly-made blades. The suggestion is that bands of men wintered at Week, which was the tool factory where they prepared their weapons for hunting on the Moor. Another suggestion is that they followed wild or semi-wild herds of cattle as the Lapps follow reindeer today. The Moor provided a suitable environment for this, and the dog, tamed by Mesolithic man, could have been used to herd as well as to hunt.

Similar sites have been recorded even more recently in the area Bridford–Christow in the Teign valley. They have not yet been fully investigated, but from them the Moor would have been accessible to hunters.

During the Mesolithic millenia the climate improved, with warmer and wetter conditions, and it reached its best about the sixth millenium BC. A rise in sea level in the same period made Britain an island, and the south-western peninsula was formed. The great plateau of Dartmoor rose to a mean height of 1,400ft above the new seas. Woodlands slowly filled the valleys, alder and oak flourishing, so that the open heath was confined to the higher levels. Through the centuries man's wandering existence continued. On the south-western highlands it must have seemed that the nomadic way of life would never end.

THE FIRST TOMBS

During the fourth millenium BC the Mesolithic culture began

15

to give way to the Neolithic or New Stone Age. The trickle of new immigrants were farmers who had domesticated cattle and grew crops. They were small, long-headed, agile people, skilled with tools. Crossing from the Continent to the coast of Devon with their seeds and stock they became the first Devon farmers. Typical villages of wattle and daub huts were established—a causewayed camp at Hembury in East Devon, and an open settlement at Hazard Hill in the valley of the Harbourne, only three miles from the edge of Dartmoor. A Neolithic house has also been excavated on the great ridge of Haldon, between Exeter and the Moor.

Later immigrants apparently settled at Week, and also near Bridford, probably mingling with and absorbing the nomadic Mesoliths in those favourable areas. Neolithic tools have been recorded on Dartmoor; significantly most of them were associated with Mesolithic finds. They were present at the two Mesolithic sites near Postbridge. At Gidleigh Common implements of Neolithic type included thirteen arrowheads and part of a polished stone axe. Leaf-shaped arrowheads at Welstor were found with Mesolithic and later flints. These tools and weapons could have been traded to Mesolithic bands still using the Moor, or have been discarded by mixed Mesolithic–Neolithic hunters or herdsmen.

A few other tools of Neolithic type have been found. A chipped flint axe came from the foot of Cawsand or Cosdon Hill, opposite Belstone (page 143), and a ground and polished stone axe was discovered at Wedlake Farm (sq 5377), Peter Tavy, as recently as 1964. Some fine leaf-arrowheads were picked up in the last century on the Moor above Okehampton (page 143). These were all isolated finds on the edge of the Moor.

It has been suggested that some settlements, eg the group of enclosures at Trowlesworthy Warren (Plym), may have been

Page 17 (above) Remnants of the chambered tomb at Corringdon Ball. The large stone lying on the ground is probably the capstone; *(below)* the ruined chambered tomb at Cuckoo Ball

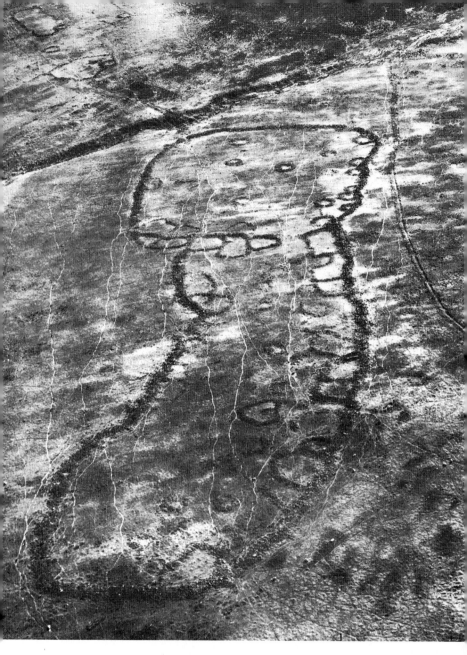

Page 18 The large double enclosure at Riders Rings looking south-west, with numerous ruined huts and stock pens. The water supply was the stream on the south side of the original small enclosure

of Neolithic origin. Evidence is lacking. No trace of any village like Hembury or Hazard Hill, no pottery of Neolithic type, no other evidence of Neolithic settlement has yet been found. The Moor may have been used for seasonal grazing— the Mesoliths would have helped as herdsmen—but probably the uplands over 900ft did not attract the early farmers.

Later waves of Neolithic people brought the art of mega-lithic building to Devon—the construction of chambered tombs covered by barrows, and used for successive burials. The chamber was formed by upright stones, sometimes with drystone walling, covered by a large stone known as a cap-stone. The so-called Spinster's Rock near Drewsteignton, two miles off the Moor, is a restored example of such a chamber; and the remnants of two exist on the south edge of the Moor.

One is the much ravaged barrow on the saddle between **Brent Fore Hill and Corringdon Ball** (page 17), two miles **north-west** of South Brent. It stands between the valleys of Avon and Glazebrook at 1,050ft above sea level. Though dominated by higher ground to north and south, the site is impressive when approached from the west. The dead were important to Neolithic man and tombs were carefully sited and built. The Corringdon Ball barrow was of the type known as Gallery Graves, ie with a single burial chamber of large stones at one end. The barrow is orientated north-west–south-east and was originally about 140ft long with a maximum width of 50–60ft over the chamber at the southern end. The barrow is shrunken and negligible and only four uprights of the chamber remain, all fallen except for one small stone. A huge flat stone on the ground nearby, 11ft long and between 1–2ft thick, may well be the capstone.

Two miles south-west of Corringdon Ball the other wrecked burial chamber lies on the slope of Cuckoo Ball (659582—page 17). Situated at a height of 950ft above sea level, its position on the hill is not remarkable; but the English Channel can be seen from it, and it appears crest-sited when approached from the south-east. Seven stones of the chamber remain, only two of them upright; the largest stands 5ft 10in high. There is no trace of a capstone and the only indication of a barrow is round the chamber. One authority (H. O. Hencken) considered that the chamber was originally covered by a long barrow, orientated north and south, and 120ft long.

Both tombs may be dated between 3000–2000 BC and pose a difficult question: who built them on these lofty sites, remote from any contemporary settlement?

Although it would be reasonable to suppose that they would be sited in relation to some community, no Neolithic village is nearer to either of them than Hazard Hill, six miles away off the Moor. The most impressive approach to Corringdon Ball is from the East Glazebrook valley, and to Cuckoo Ball from the valley of the little Lud Brook. These valleys seem unlikely sites for Neolithic settlement. There remains the possibility that settlers at Hazard Hill carried the bodies of their leaders all the way to the uplands for burial, perhaps when bringing up their stock for summer grazing. This is not altogether a satisfactory theory, but it is the best that can be offered at present.

Both barrows are totally wrecked and cannot compare visually with the better known Neolithic tombs of Wessex and the Cotswolds. But one thing is certain: they are the oldest constructions of man to remain on Dartmoor. For the first time the granite had been used to house the dead. It was an indication of things to come.

In the light of present knowledge, the Neolithic period therefore left few traces. The mingled Mesolithic–Neolithic hunters and herdsmen probably continued to use the Moor into the second millennium BC, and even so recently, man had made little impression on the great plateau. The only signs of him were a few seasonal wanderers, the tools and weapons they abandoned, and two solitary long barrows in the south. Though the blanket bog was slowly beginning to form—vegetation decomposing in wet conditions and being partly carbonised—the climate was still at its best. The stage was set for the reception of a new culture, and for the first colonisation of the Moor.

2

INTRODUCTION TO THE
BRONZE AGE

Metal implements began to reach Dartmoor early in the second millenium BC. They were brought by small groups of immigrants known as the Beaker people who had erupted from Spain and spread rapidly over central and western Europe. Their name is derived from their characteristic pottery: small drinking cups with an elongated S outline, well-fired, and decorated with patterns of incised lines. The people themselves were round-headed, powerfully built, and skilled with the bow. In contrast to the Neolithic farmers they were herdsmen and hunters rather than cultivators, and they buried their dead singly. When they reached Devon the Mesolithic–Neolithic inhabitants were quickly dominated and the first settlements established on the Moor.

Stone axes, flint knives and arrowheads were still the principal implements, but some of the Beaker people, probably the leaders, owned copper blades or the superior bronze blades made of copper with a ten to fifteen per cent tin alloy. These had been in use in Europe for several centuries. By contact with the Continent, and by discovery of the rich metallic sources in south-west Britain and in Ireland, the Beaker people introduced Bronze Age culture to Britain. The centuries following their arrival were to be the most important in Dartmoor's prehistory.

Although the Beaker people were the first to settle on the Moor, none of their settlements have been found and nothing is known of their domestic life. Their burials in small, round mounds—with rows of stones often marking the approach to them—have been identified. They also built circles of standing stones, some of which remain. These indicate that the main area of settlement was in a broad band stretching diagonally north-east–south-west from the North Teign watershed and across the upper valleys of the Darts to the Plym (Fig 2).

The monuments attributed to the Beaker people reveal megalithic influence. In Wessex they did not destroy existing monuments, such as the earliest Stonehenge, but developed them. The Dartmoor settlers came from or through Wessex, and their monuments also should be regarded as the product of mixed Beaker–Neolithic cultures.

Small immigrations continued throughout early Bronze Age times and the sparse population must have increased sufficiently to hold its own in the Moor valleys. The trade routes established by the Beaker people were followed in due course by other settlers from Wessex and by people coming direct from the Continent to the south coast and settling in valleys such as the Erme and Avon, where evidence of Beaker presence is comparatively slight. Very little is known in detail about this long period of trade and settlement. Eventually Bronze culture became firmly established and the moorland communities settled down to a comparatively stable existence.

The Moor offered much that Bronze Age man needed: large areas of grazing for his animals and abundant water; also peat and wood for fuel; soil for small arable plots and, in some areas, suitable ground for cultivation on a slightly larger scale; and surface stone to house the living and the dead. Such conditions ensured that no dramatic change in custom or

23

FIG. 2.

BEAKER SITES

& Standing Stones

□ Cemeteries
+ Sanctuaries
o Circles
❘ Standing Stones

economy took place until the climate deteriorated, early in the first millenium BC.

The Moor could not supply all essential material for weapons and household goods. There was wood for axe-handles and spear-handles and for bows; clay, shale and slate could be obtained locally, though off the granite; bronze and flint were acquired by trade. Ireland was rich in gold and copper, Devon and Cornwall rich in tin. Trade flourished all over the south and west of Britain and into Ireland and Spain. There is some evidence that Cornish tin was exported in Bronze Age times, but the question whether tin was also taken from Dartmoor has, until recently, been argued without evidence.

Many of the Bronze Age settlements on the Moor were concentrated in the valleys where alluvial tin would have been available. Medieval tinners were attracted to the same valleys. Prehistoric man would have taken tin ore from the surface gravels, and it is arguable that later streaming and mining have obliterated all trace of surface working. The using up of surface deposits could account for the spread of settlements up the valleys—the settlers moved on when the supply at any place was exhausted. This is an attractive theory. Unfortunately, no prehistoric smelting site has been found. Until the excavation of a settlement on Dean Moor in 1954-5 no evidence at all had been recorded of prehistoric tin-working on Dartmoor. At Dean Moor a pebble of tin ore (cassiterite) was found in one hut, and a drop of tin slag in another. The tin ore could have been taken from nearby gravels, indicating that the ore was recognised. The slag must have been brought into the hut accidentally from a smelting place, but the site of this has not been found. Until a smelting site is located, or the special qualities of Dartmoor tin are identified in a prehistoric tool or weapon, the proof of extraction or smelting on the Moor during the Bronze Age is lacking. Yet it does not seem realistic that Dartmoor deposits were ignored while extraction was going on in Cornwall.

Long occupation by Bronze Age communities is evidenced by an astonishing number of remains. No other area of the same size surpasses Dartmoor in this respect, not even the chalk downs of Wessex with their superior cultures. None of the Moor sites were of the magnitude of Avebury or Stonehenge, but many are still sited impressively. A road and village disrupt the great design of Avebury, and Stonehenge is held in the cleft of a busy trunk road and another highway. The remains on the Moor are in valleys of lively and beautiful rivers, and on hill slopes surrounded by unbroken miles of moorland. In the south and west the views extend to the English Channel and far into Cornwall. The face of the Moor has been altered by forest clearance, by medieval settlement and mining, by modern industry, roads, enclosure, afforestation, reservoirs; but in many places the environment of the Bronze Age is comparatively unchanged.

A hundred years of exploration has been necessary even to list the Moor's Bronze Age remains. Up to the middle of last century general descriptions and mythical interpretations had sufficed. In 1862 the Devonshire Association was founded and one of its first tasks was to organise exploration on the Moor and the recording of results. In 1878 it appointed a Barrow Committee to investigate burials, and in 1893 a Dartmoor Exploration Committee. The members of these two bodies (R. H. Worth and Robert Burnard were outstanding among them) surveyed, investigated and recorded the prehistoric remains. More than a hundred barrows or cairns were described and planned, twenty settlements explored, innumerable stone rows and circles examined and measured. Though many of the investigations were unsatisfactory by today's standard, they paved the way for a modern approach to the multiplicity of remains. Without the immense efforts of these enthusiasts, few sites would be marked on the OS maps and no coherent account of the prehistoric Moor could be attempted.

The most numerous and important remains are the settlements. In no other area in England have so many relics of Bronze Age habitations survived. On the east side of the Moor they spread from the slopes of Cosdon in the north (not far from the Mesolithic–Neolithic sites at Week) right down to Horridge Common. There are scattered settlements surviving in the valleys of the Darts and their tributaries. The greatest concentration lies in the south and south-west valleys —Avon, Erme, Yealm, Plym and their tributaries—with some pushed far up the Tavy, Walkham, and Lyd on the west side (Fig 3).

Three main types of settlement have been distinguished. *Enclosed settlements* were groups of huts surrounded by substantial walls, mainly curved and with rounded angles. Locally these are called Pounds, but as the term also implies enclosures solely for cattle and ponies, the modern name is more explicit. Most of them were small, with less than half a dozen buildings, but a few were much larger, eg twenty-four at Grimspound and over thirty at Riders Rings, though these buildings were not all habitations. Sometimes the enclosures were multiple, as at Yes Tor Bottom (two) and Legis Tor (four). They were not forts, but the homes of herdsmen. At night, and when conditions prevented grazing, cattle and sheep were impounded to prevent straying and for protection against predators. Calving, rearing, gelding and slaughtering, must also have taken place in or near the enclosures.

The second type of settlement consisted of open groups

FIG 3
BRONZE AGE SETTLEMEN[ ]

○ Enclosed Settlement[s]
× Villages
● Farms

of huts best referred to as *Villages*. The huts were often connected by low walls to form irregular encloures. These also were the homes of predominantly stock-raising people. Generally they were larger groups than the enclosed settlements.

Evidence of cultivation has been found in enclosed settlements and villages in the form of querns and grain rubbers. The identification of actual corn plots in or near settlements is difficult. Judging by the terrain where these types of settlement existed, the plots would have been very small, and cultivated by hoeing or digging rather than by ploughing. Cereals were only a supplementary item in the diet.

In both these types of settlement the huts were roughly circular with an internal diameter rarely exceeding 25ft. Walls were of earth and/or small stones, up to 5ft thick, with large slabs of undressed stone on the inside. The spaces between the slabs were filled with dry-stone masonry. Large stones, and sometimes banks of earth, supported the exterior face of the wall. The floor of the huts was below ground level, top-soil being removed, and the sub-soil levelled where the site was sloping. On Dartmoor a level site even for one or two huts was difficult to find.

Entrances faced in any direction except north and northwest, ie away from the direct blast of the winds which, in Worth's words, 'are the greatest enemies of all living things on the Moor'. Doorways were low and narrow, not usually more than 3ft high or wide. The entrance and step down into the hut were paved, the approach to the entrance cobbled. Sometimes the doorway was screened by an extension to the hut wall.

Roofs of turf, heather, or rushes, were normally conical, supported by a centre post. In larger huts—say of 15ft and over in diameter—a ring of smaller posts between centre and wall was necessary to bear the weight of the roof. Rafter ends were wedged into the wall. Branches of hazel and birch laid across the rafters served as purlins to support the thatch. The general construction of the huts appears to have changed little during Bronze Age times, though excavation has revealed variations in interior planning.

The third type of settlement was the *Farm*—huts associated with fields, indicating more emphasis on arable farming. They occupied areas where soil and climate made this possible, and it is noticeable that these areas hardly overlap those where villages and enclosed settlements were established. The farmhouses were similar in plan and construction to the huts already described, but usually bigger, up to 30ft and more in diameter, and often made with larger slabs.

Within each type of settlement considerable variation appears, as though each site was adapted independently. All types of settlement co-existed. In some cases an occupation date can be hazarded from pottery finds, but accurate dating is not yet possible. The overall picture is of long periods of occupation. Comparatively few settlements have been excavated, and up to World War II the pick-axe, shovel and garden sieve were the tools used. In many huts only charcoal and cooking stones were recovered. Unwittingly, the early diggers ignored or destroyed evidence. Since World War II only one enclosed settlement (Dean Moor) and part of a farm (Kestor) have been excavated and recorded using modern techniques.

Many huts exist which cannot be included in the three types described. They are scattered all over the Moor except in the north-west. Possibly some are relics of large groups and some the homes of independent settlers and herdsmen.

Next in importance to the houses of the living are the 'houses' of the dead. Unfortunately, any connection between burial sites and settlements is difficult to find. Most of the burials were earlier than the surviving settlements, and it seems that the pastoralists and farmers of main Bronze Age times gradually gave up making elaborate tombs and observing the rituals of their ancestors.

The Beaker people introduced individual burial, in modest round barrows. Those on Dartmoor were of the simplest kind, without ditches or encircling banks; but they often had substantial stones forming a closeset or open circle round the burial. Barrows were made of stone and/or earth and turf, and as surface stone was available so freely on the Moor, most of them were mainly or solely of stone. Confusion may be avoided by referring to them generally as *cairns*, the term used on OS maps except in a few instances where they are known or described as barrows or tumuli, irrespective of construction. They covered single burials and rarely exceeded 30ft in diameter. There are much larger cairns visible today, up to 120ft in diameter, but these are exceptional.

Though some cairns have not yielded traces of a burial, they were generally built to mark and protect either pits and shallow depressions in the sub-soil, or the small stone boxes known as *kists*. The pits were small, sometimes covered by stones. They were for cremated ashes, and burnt bone has been identified in some of them.

Most kists were large enough to hold a body in a crouched or trussed position, which was the original Beaker custom, but some were used for cremations. They were of unworked slabs forming two sides, two ends, and a coverstone. The walls rested in the sub-soil, the coverstone was above ground-level. The Dartmoor kists are a unique collection of pre-historic tombs.

The *stone rows* associated with Beaker burials were single, double and triple lines of unworked stones leading to cairns. They appear to mark ceremonial or symbolic approaches to important tombs. Normally they went uphill to the cairn, which was often false crested when approached from that direction. The alignment of rows was governed by the slope of the hill, and the larger stones in them were placed nearest to the cairn. Fully-defined rows vary in length from thirty-five yards to over two miles.

Two significant shapes have been noticed among the stones in rows: pillars, and slabs with flat or triangular tops. Similar shapes can be recognised in stones encircling burials. Without artificial shaping this indicates careful selection and recalls another Beaker monument, the West Kennet Avenue, between Avebury and Overton Hill sanctuary in Wiltshire. That also has stones of two distinct shapes, pillar-like and broad, arranged in facing pairs. These shapes are believed to be fertility symbols, representing male and female. It is possible that a similar idea was brought to Dartmoor by the Beaker people. The dead were important in their beliefs. One theory is that the rows were vaginal symbols—the body which emerged through a vagina at birth was returned at death along a stone vagina to a cairn–womb. Perhaps the cairns were visited on anniversaries, or other special occasions, with processions up the rows and ceremonies to renew contact with the powerful dead. Few facts are likely to emerge from excavation. The rows are a local type of monument not found in such numbers elsewhere in Britain and are as unique as the Dartmoor kists.

The *stone circles,* also attributed to the Beaker people, were another type of monument of which the exact significance is unknown. They should not be confused with the circles of stones round burials. It is clear that they formed imporant ceremonial sites, erected also in Cornwall (eg the Hurlers on Bodmin Moor), and in Somerset. They vary in diameter between 60–120ft and, except in one or two instances, the stones do not exceed 4ft above ground. An analogy with the inner circles at Avebury is apparent. Their use on Dartmoor probably continued long after the Beaker people had blended with the natives they had dominated and with later immigrants. Gradually, respect for Beaker ritual declined and the sacred sites were ignored, rather as some churches and churchyards are neglected today.

Similarly, the single *Standing stones*, in the past called menhirs, were probably objects of importance over a long period. Large upright stones are present in many stone rows and in at least one of the circles, but there are a few isolated stones, selected and erected with care, which are not apparently associated with other remains.

Compared with the great number of remains, the finds of tools, weapons and domestic objects have been few. Hundreds of tombs have produced no identifiable bone, only a few samples of burnt bone. No bones of cattle, sheep or other animals have survived in the settlements. The acid soil of the Moor, over long periods, destroys bone and severely damages metal. The Beaker grave-goods were few and poor, and later the custom of burying objects with the dead was gradually abandoned. Add to these facts the merciless pillaging and destruction through the centuries, and perhaps the scarcity of objects to survive is not surprising. All types of remains have been sacrificed to make and mend buildings, newtake walls, leats and roads.

The surviving relics reveal the affinities of the Moormen with Beaker and Bronze Age peoples of other parts of Devon, and of Cornwall and Wessex. Daily life in the settlements must have been similar to that of pastoralists everywhere.

Tending cattle and sheep was the main task, and meat, milk, wool and hides formed the basis for survival. Pottery, and horn and stone tools, were made by hand; small plots, and in limited areas fields, were tilled for cereals; and the men were hunters as well as herdsmen. Metal tools and weapons made tree-felling and hunting easier than before.

But life on Dartmoor had some special characteristics—the granite-walled buildings, so different in durability from mud, reed and wooden structures; the almost certain extraction of tin; and the unsuitablity of most of the terrain for ploughs or war-chariots—these were the factors that contributed to the formation of a peculiarly local and self-sufficient society. In spite of their tin, the settlers in the high valleys were rather remote from the main trade routes and the main centres of Bronze Age culture in Britain.

Today the ruins of their homes and monuments litter the Moor; and their rough pastures, though reduced by medieval and modern enclosure, still provide extensive grazing grounds. A wanderer across the uplands and the deep valleys is made vividly aware of the early Moormen.

The double enclosure near Yealm Steps looking east. Hut foundations can be seen outside the enclosure walls to north and south

Page 36 (above) Five of the small enclosures at Trowlesworthy, two joined together. They lie on the slope above the Lee Moor leat, which cuts the top left corner of the picture. Three enclosures below the leat complete the group; (below) Bronze Age pottery (left) restored cup with 'dimple' decoration found near the Dewerstone as recently as 1960; (right) restored bucket-shaped vessel from Raddick Hill, with incised chevron decoration, found by Robert Burnard in 1896

3
THE ENCLOSED SETTLEMENTS

Enclosed hut groups are the characteristic type of settlement on Dartmoor. Remains of more than a hundred still exist. Three-quarters of them are in the south and south-west valleys of Avon, Erme, Yealm, Plym and their tributaries, half being concentrated on the Avon and Plym. The remainder lie scattered in the area of the Darts and their tributaries, with a few on the west side of the Moor and in the north-east. They are situated mainly between 1,100–1,400ft above sea level, on slopes exposed to the warm, rain-bearing, south-westerly winds. Grazing, and water for men and cattle, were readily available near all sites. The best known example is Grimspound at the head of a feeder stream of the West Webburn, a tributary of the Dart, but it is not typical. Most enclosed settlements were much smaller, and it is situated outside the area of the main groups. Its comparatively good state of preservation, some restoration, and easy access, have combined to give it prominence.

AVON

Twenty-nine settlements have been recorded in the valley of the Avon and its moorland tributary, the Bala Brook. They extend for some three miles up both sides of the Avon, in groups on the slopes between the feeder streams. Most of them are small, with fewer than ten huts, and over half of them have only three huts or less. It is the larger ones, of course, which have attracted attention.

Riders Rings was an exceptionally large settlement, on the right bank, at an altitude of 1,150–1,250ft (page 18). The site is a gentle slope below the crest of the hill which rises 300ft from the river to Zeal Plains. In spite of its devastated condition it was clearly an important and impressive place. The views from it across the valley to the open moor, and south to Black and Shipley Tors and over a large part of the South Hams, are memorable.

It consisted of two enclosures, one roughly square and a larger one roughly oblong in plan, sharing a party wall. An area of six acres was enclosed containing more than thirty buildings. The larger enclosure, as in the case of other multiple settlements, had been built on to the smaller, and indicates an expanding community. A nearby feeder stream of the Avon supplied water, except during very dry periods.

A limited exploration of two huts in the larger enclosure, and of a section of the wall—the best preserved part of the wall, including an original entrance—was carried out by Worth in August 1930. He found that the wall was faced on both sides with small blocks of pink felsite, the form of granite available nearby. It was filled with small stones and was six to seven feet thick. The original height can only be surmised. It must have been high enough to keep cattle in and predators out, with or without some form of palisade on top. Most settlements had walls which seem a great deal more substantial than was necessary for these purposes, but no doubt the builders knew what they were doing. Hut walls also were often of massive construction.

Built on to the inside of the enclosure wall were several

small yards, presumably stock pens. A trench cut across one of them revealed no sign of habitation, only natural soil. Traces of similar pens will be noted at other sites on the Moor.

Some of the huts were free-standing, some joined to the pen walls. The two selected for excavation were of the latter type. The first was 20ft in diameter and produced only some charcoal and cooking stones, ie water-worn stones suitable for heating. The second hut, 24ft in diameter, produced charcoal, cooking stones, flint chips and a broken whetstone of red grit. There were also some fragments of pottery described as being 'of the usual Dartmoor type'. Unfortunately they were not photographed or preserved.

The second hut to be examined had one unusual feature. The hearth was 4ft directly inside the entrance. It was shielded from the entrance draught by a slab of granite about a foot high above ground-level which leant slightly inwards and was held in position by a packing of small stones. No similar hearth has been found in any other hut, the hearths usually being near the centre, or close to the wall opposite, or on either side of, the entrance.

Exploration of the Rings was confined to a week—far too short a period for any detailed work to be attempted. With modern techniques the excavation of two huts alone would have required several weeks. No dates can at present be given for the construction or occupation of the enclosures. It was a large pastoral settlement of the Bronze Age, the largest enclosed settlement recorded on the Moor except for a single vast enclosure on Broad Down (East Dart).

A quarter of a mile across the river valley from the Rings, at the foot of Grippers Hill (681649) are the remains of another multiple settlement. The 1,050ft contour passes through the site and it is therefore lower and nearer to the

river than the Rings. This settlement was examined and surveyed in 1954, prior to its disturbance by quarrying in connection with the building of the Avon Dam.

The site was carefully chosen. It is on a fairly level part of
the hill, with small outcrops of rock on the lower side, and
the slope above rising steeply and covered in boulders.
Nearly all the walls were found to be completely ruined, and
the hut walls in bad condition, but four enclosures in a line
north-west–south-east were traced. The northernmost enclosure had only a segment of boundary wall, and one hut,
and may not have been an enclosure at all but merely a
collecting place for animals. The two central enclosures had
had substantial walls to contain stock, and wide entrances
uphill towards the grazing grounds. They were the first
structures to be built. They appear to have contained only
one hut each, presumably for the herdsman in charge.
Ruined walls inside one of them indicated stock pens, as at
the Rings, and small huts for other herdsmen may have been
joined to these. The southernmost enclosure had less-
substantial walls and five huts. It was apparently an area
reserved for human habitation rather than for impounding
and tending stock. At the Rings, no such division is noticeable, the huts and stock pens being mixed in both enclosures.

Outside the walls of the enclosures were four more huts.
This feature of external huts associated with an enclosed
settlement is found at many other sites.

The three complete enclosures have a total area of less
than two acres. They represent the home of a community
considerably smaller, and probably less prosperous, than
that at the Rings. No excavation was carried out, and again
no period of occupation more precise than the Bronze Age
can be given.

Three settlements were situated on Dean Moor, on the

hillside rising from the Avon to the west of the Brockhill stream. It is a gentle, south-facing slope, a typical Dartmoor site. Coming out of the gloom of his hut, the early Moorman would have seen around him the sombre hills shutting in the windings of the river and its feeder streams. The valley would have been more wooded than now, but in any case the construction of the Avon reservoir has altered the landscape. Paradoxically, the access road which had to be made to the dam site enabled a full-scale excavation on Dean Moor to be carried out.

In two seasons (1954–5) the settlement nearest the river,

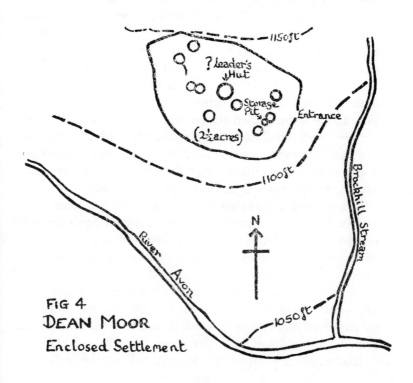

FiG 4
DEAN MOOR
Enclosed Settlement

41

where the waters of the reservoir at high level now lap, was excavated under the supervision of Lady Fox.

The single enclosure (Fig 4) is less than half a mile north of the Grippers Hill compounds and is at 1,100–1,150ft above sea level. It had an area of two and a half acres and contained ten huts. The original entrance was on the east side, sixty yards from the Brockhill stream, the water supply. The wall on that side was massive, 10ft thick, and on the south side 9ft. It was faced externally with large boulders. Probably it was not more than 4ft high, sufficient to keep stock in, and with a palisade or hedge on top to keep wild animals out.

Seven free-standing huts and one double hut were excavated. They were all roughly circular, the single huts with diameters between twenty and twenty-eight feet, the semi-detacheds rather smaller with diameters of 16ft. The latter had separate roofs and entrances and were divided by a substantial party wall which was buttressed at the lower end. All the hut walls had been substantial, from four to seven feet thick. Large slabs formed the inner face, backed with a core of stones, and small stones were roughly laid to form the outer face. Entrances faced east (four), south-east, south-west (three) and west, so placed that they did not confront one another. An unexpected desire for privacy is indicated.

Entrances did not exceed 3ft in width. Four of them were screened by walls or boulders on the north side, to keep out the cold winds blowing down the valley from the north-west. The approaches were cobbled up to 7ft outside, and stepped where they lay uphill.

Central post holes, and ring post holes of varying number, were found in nearly all huts, indicating conical roofs. A semi-detached hut without a central post hole may have had an oval roof, though a centre post was not structurally essential where the rafters were supported by the wall and ring posts. On the sloping site the walls on the lower side were usually built up to make a more or less level base all round for the rafters; and the floor inside was partly levelled by excavation and packing

For the first time, the huts of an enclosed settlement were fully excavated and recorded. Though superficially similar, each hut was different in one way or another, revealing an individual adaptation to family requirements and to its position in the enclosure. These variations, and the finds in the huts, give the most intimate picture of Bronze Age life on Dartmoor so far available.

In most of the huts the floor was clean on one side of the entrance, where the family slept, and messy on the other, where the hearth was found and all dirty chores were done. One hearth was central, two were at the back of the hut in line with the entrance, and the remainder were to one side or the other between centre and wall but always in a lower quarter of the hut. This positioning would have helped to keep the sleeping quarters clean. One hearth consisted of a bedded stone with a fender of upright stones. All the floor in one hut was cobbled with small pieces of granite, another had patches of cobbles and paving, another some large patches of paving only. The inhabitants squatted on the floor, though surface boulders left inside one hut could have been used as seats.

Separate sleeping quarters were found in three huts. One of the semi-detached had a recess or extension on the higher side, 5–6ft deep, and large enough for two people to sleep in, curled up. Although no bones have survived, the hut dwellers were almost certainly of smaller stature than present-day Devonians. Two of the single huts had inner rooms. Natural boulders formed the partition in one, and the other had had a turf wall on stone foundations. Paving slabs marked the entrance to the inner room from the main part of the hut. This shutting off of sleeping space, like the positioning of hut entrances, reveals a respect for privacy not formerly associated with the early Moormen.

Cooking holes were found in some huts (ie holes in which meat could be cooked with heated stones), and soakaways or refuse pits in others. Three huts produced evidence of pottery making—patches of clay trodden into the floor and a ball of yellow clay, and in one hut wall a recess containing clay waste, probably a clay store.

A special feature was an underground storage pit, partly quarried from the granite, and protected by a stone wall built out from a hut. It was reached from the hut entrance passage and was possibly a grain store. The wall round the pit acted as a north screen for the hut entrance.

In another hut a small wall niche, in the same quarter as the hearth, may have been a cupboard for food or tools, or even a shrine for the family idol. A similar cupboard with stone top and sides was recorded some sixty years previously in a hut at Cullacombe Head, Shapley Common (see Chapter 4).

As important as the hut detail were the finds, collected from walls and floors with meticulous care. Some huts produced very few objects, the expected result of most Dartmoor exploration. But other huts produced unique finds.

First place is usually given to pottery, but at Dean Moor the finding of a pebble of tin ore and a blob of tin slag takes precedence. It must be repeated—they are the only evidence of prehistoric tin-working on Dartmoor so far discovered. Both might have been missed altogether by less dedicated workers. The tin slag was no bigger than a large pin-head. It was found among the charcoal round a hearth, together with the shell of a hazel nut.

Another unique find was of two small carnelian beads in the largest—probably the leader's—hut. They were lying towards the centre on the surface of the floor, immediately below the top turf formed since occupation ceased. They therefore appear to have been dropped by the inhabitants when the hut was abandoned. Carnelian stone is present in the South West; but the beads were perforated, and the skill required to drill this very hard gem-stone indicates an origin far away from Dean Moor. They may have been acquired from traders along the south coast. Few of these beads have been found anywhere in England.

Finds of pottery were in poor condition and some fragments had to be left exposed to dry and harden before they could be picked up and sent away for treatment. They all came from straight-sided vessels of coarse texture, not exceeding 8in in diameter. They were made by hand, fired over open hearths with the fire heaped round them, and mostly dark brown in colour. They are comparable to some previous finds on Dartmoor. Examples show characteristic flat rims, which permitted the vessel to be placed upside down during manufacture, or for draining or storing when in use. Decoration was by incised lines and groves, made with a rounded point of wood or bone; and by impressions of twisted and plaited cords. One fragment was of exceptional interest. It showed a flat band or cordon with part of a strap handle extending below it. Pots found on Dartmoor previously were lifted by lugs. But generally the pottery resembles finds elsewhere in the South West, with flat rims and cordons, incised and cord decoration, and lugs. It belongs stylistically to main Bronze Age times (c 1400–900 BC), but this would not necessarily have prevented it from being made or used during the next two or three centuries.

Broken whetstones for sharpening metal implements were

found in all huts. Some had grooves, the result of use for pointing. Grooved whetstones are not common finds anywhere in England, and these are the first recorded from Dartmoor. A plain one was similar to that found at Riders Rings. The stones were all water-worn and came from nearby stream beds.

Evidence of arable farming, apart from the underground storage pit already described, was provided by part of a saddle-quern and a worn grain-rubber. The latter had a thumb grip on one side. The lower part of the enclosure appeared suitable for cultivation, but no evidence of this was obtained. The settlement was predominantly pastoral, and a shale spindle whorl implied that sheep as well as cattle were kept. Shale was available in the South Hams.

Finally, embedded in the core of a hut wall and sealed under its floor, an unexpected discovery: 50lb of iron ore in small pieces. The position of these pieces, and their association with Bronze Age pottery fragments, showed that the deposit was made in prehistoric times. It was good quality ore, without any sign of attempts at smelting. This confirmed that the date of the settlement was pre-Iron Age. The inhabitants of Dean Moor recognised the ore and carried it home, but apparently did not know how to extract iron.

To summarise the results of this excavation: important evidence was collected as to construction of huts, economy, and dating. All records of previous explorations of settlements must be reviewed in the light of the knowledge obtained at Dean Moor.

No other settlements in the upper Avon valley have been excavated or even surveyed in detail.

GLAZEBROOK

Five settlements survive in this short valley. A hut in the

southernmost, near Scad Brook (666599), was investigated in 1952. It had a diameter of 16ft, and an entrance facing south-east. The wall was lined inside with large granite slabs. The hearth was central. Charcoal, cooking stones, three pieces of flint and fragments of coarse pottery were found. The pottery was without decoration but similar in texture and appearance to pottery found in other enclosed settlements. An unusual discovery was a small piece of black haematite (iron ore), smooth and shiny as though it had been used for polishing. As at Dean Moor, the inhabitants knew the ore and, in this instance, had apparently found a use for it in its natural state.

ERME

A score of settlements exist in the Erme valley but only a few of them have more than three huts. None have been excavated, and no finds have been recorded. Apart from spoliation they offer a virgin field for the archaeologist. Many, however, are sited a long way from the nearest road and are difficult to reach with the equipment necessary for a full scale dig.

The pattern of settlement was similar to that on the Avon, extending for miles up the valley. The remotest group is on Brown Heath, between Red Lake and Hook Lake, five miles across the Moor from Wrangaton. Three enclosures lie close to the river, on a south-west slope, and within less than half a mile of each other.

The northernmost, known from subsequent use as Erme Pound, has the ruins of a few huts in its higher part. The enclosure wall runs for a short distance within a few yards of the river, and is about 4ft high along most of its length, with an entrance in good condition on the south-east side. Impressive to look at, its present state is due to rebuilding in historic times when it was used for mustering and impounding cattle and ponies. Probably only some of the foundations are pre-historic. Ruined buildings and several small enclosures near-by are also of comparatively recent origin, so that Erme Pound has little prehistoric significance. The two other settlements on Brown Heath are more interesting and characteristic.

They are roughly-circular enclosures, the lower one less than 100yd from the junction of Hook Lake with the Erme, the other 150yd further up the slope. The walls are ruined but well defined, many large stones remaining, especially in the higher and larger settlement where there are also traces of stock pens built on to the wall. Remains of huts are difficult to see. Probably each enclosure had three or four in its lower quarter. Outside, between the settlements, the remains of five huts are clear.

Close to the south-east angle of the higher settlement is a ruined cairn marked by a circle of stones 30ft in diameter. Worth recollected that there had been a kist in the centre, but no trace of this, except perhaps for some packing stones, remains. Leading up the slope to the cairn is a double stone row which begins against the east wall of the lower enclosure. It seems that the row originally may have extended closer to Hook Lake, and the builders of the enclosure destroyed part of it. Settlements close to monuments were intrusive. During the Bronze Age, burial customs gradually became simpler, and existing cairns and rows ceased to be respected. The settlements on Brown Heath are an early example of Dart-moor practicality: the herdsmen were not going to be denied a good site by a tomb and its ceremonial approach.

William Crossing in his *Guide to Dartmoor* described the view from the hut groups on Brown Heath as '... a scene of desolation. Not even a tor is visible, only long stretches of heath with the great ridge of Stalldon rising high to the south. The Erme pursuing its course through the long valley alone gives life to the picture. But the seclusion of this part of the moor endows it with a certain charm...' The description remains valid. Even on a fine summer day the surrounding hills are sombre and desolate. It is a good place for contemplating the environment of Bronze Age man, bearing in mind that the valley was then more wooded than today.

A group of twelve enclosures on the south-east slope of Stalldon (sqs 6361/6461), though much denuded, merits attention. The site is a fine one, 875–1,000ft above sea level and looking down to the deep valley of the Erme. The enclosures are spread along the slope for some 800yd. Each has one or two huts, and there are traces of a score of huts outside. A semi-detached pair is unusually sited with the floor of one hut 5ft below the level of the other. A modern track through the middle of the group, and newtake walls nearby, account for the devastation of this remarkable cluster.

YEALM

Some of the eight settlements on the Yealm and its feeder streams have interesting features. North-east of Dendles Wood a semi-circular enclosure without huts (624624) is built on to a larger enclosure with sixteen huts—probably an example of a large external stock pen. The inhabited enclosure has a stream running through it. Two other examples of such a convenient water supply will be noted later.

A settlement near Yealm Steps (620636—page 35) consists of a small enclosure with five huts to which a larger enclosure with sixteen huts was added. There are five huts outside to the north and more than a dozen spread down the slope to the south, making an impressive group. The hut walls were built of rather small stones, which may account for their overgrown condition; but some hut entrances have prominent jambs, and the smaller enclosure has a clearly defined entrance facing south. Many large boulders litter the slope down to the river, but they are of unsuitable size and shape for the facing of hut walls.

PLYM

With the remains of two dozen enclosed settlements the Plym is next in importance to the Avon. Most of them lie close to the river and its feeder streams in the three-mile stretch from the Blackabrook up to Lower Hartor. None have been excavated this century, but in 1895–6 Worth conducted an exploration with significant results near Legis Tor (569652—Fig 5).

The settlement consists of four enclosures on a south-west slope on the north bank of the river. Part of the wall is missing where the low cliff above the river has eroded, but the layout can be seen clearly from the slopes below Little Trowlesworthy Tor on the opposite bank. First, a small enclosure (A) of under half an acre was built, with one hut astride its northern wall. Next, a larger enclosure (B) over an acre in extent was added on the west side of A. This contained no hut, but there was one outside the enclosure and connected to it by a short wall. To A and B was added a much larger enclosure (C), over two and a half acres, containing eight to ten huts. Finally, perhaps for cultivation or the better tending of stock, a small yard or paddock (D) was carved out of C by erecting a wall across its south-east corner. Two huts on this wall may have been in existence when it was built. A curious half-hut on the same wall was perhaps the remains of one abandoned when the wall went up. All this indicates the expansion of a thriving settlement.

Worth examined eight huts inside the enclosures and five of these yielded important finds. The huts varied in diameter

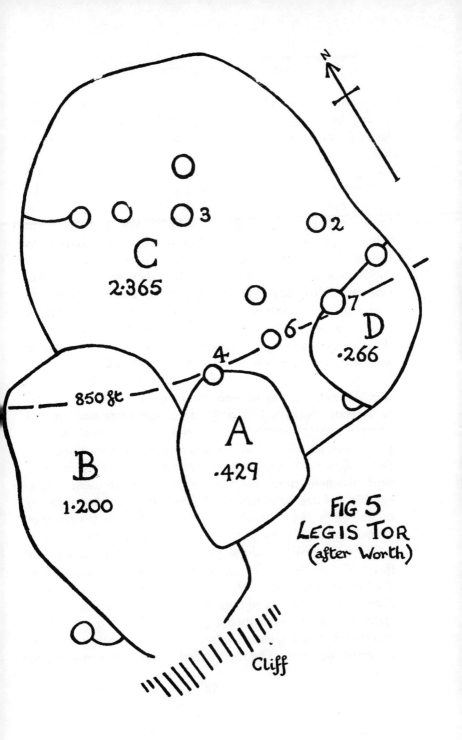

FIG 5
LEGIS TOR
(after Worth)

between 13ft and 21ft, a section of each being paved. This arrangement seems to correspond with the 'clean areas' of the Dean Moor huts. The entrances were usually on the south side, one paved and another with two steps down into the hut still in position. Apart from some good flint flakes, and a whetstone with an unfinished hole in it, the finds included a broken spindle whorl of baked clay. This was the first to be found on Dartmoor, and the only one discovered in a hut until others were found at Kestor and Dean Moor more than half a century later.

Stones had fallen from the wall in two huts, crushing but preserving fragments of pottery vessels; and in two others fragments were found in storage or cooking pits. These pieces, and the spindle whorl, whetstone, and flint flakes, make up the most interesting collection found on Dartmoor before World War II. The vessels had heavy rims and broad cordons, one cordon curiously concave in shape, with square lifting lugs. Decoration was limited to the space between rim and cordon and consisted of fingertip impressions and incised chevrons. An example of broken-line or stabbed chevron pattern, made with a comb, was a rare find for Dartmoor. At Dean Moor no finger patterns were found; at Legis Tor no cord ornamentation; otherwise the pottery from them is comparable—coarse hand-made ware with decoration mainly by incised lines. Such vessels were typical of main Bronze Age times in the South West.

Across the river, on the slopes of Little Trowlesworthy Tor (page 36), an interesting group was surveyed before World War II. It is similar to the group of enclosures on Stalldon (Erme) and at the same height above sea level. There were eight enclosures, two joined together; all less than an acre in extent. They had one to six huts each, and another ten huts were outside them. The huts varied in size between 15ft and

Page 53 More than twenty of the ruined huts at Standon village, some with connecting walls forming irregular enclosures

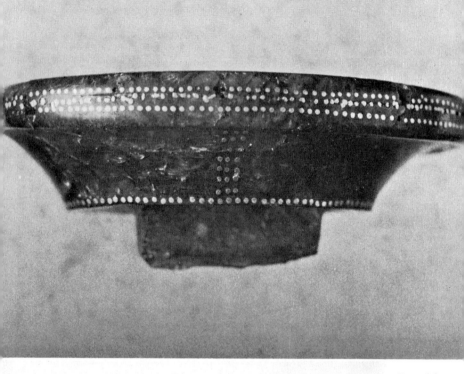

*Page 54
(above)*
Amber
pommel of a
dagger,
studded with
gold pins,
from a cairn
on Hamel-
down. Found
in 1872, it w
unfortunately
destroyed in
an air raid
during World
War II; *(left*
restored urn,
its overhang-
ing rim
decorated with
horizontal
and oblique
lines made by
impressing a
twisted cord,
recovered in
1900 from a
cairn on
Hurston
Ridge

26ft in diameter. It was suggested at one time that the enclosures might be 'lynchetted', ie that the accumulation of earth inside the lower walls was due to cultivation. But storms wash soil downhill naturally, especially where trodden by cattle, and the earth deposits cannot be accepted as proof of tilling. No cultivated plots have so far been traced in an enclosed settlement.

At Trowlesworthy, the huts and enclosures are mostly in poor condition having been interfered with when the area became a warren in medieval times and also when the Lee Moor leat was constructed through the group; but one enclosure above the leat is well defined and has substantial remains of huts.

Another group comparable to Trowlesworthy, not far away on Shaugh Moor (sq 5563), was surveyed in 1959. Seven enclosures, two joined together, had a total of twenty-eight buildings in or around them. Some of the buildings were store and cattle sheds. This settlement and those at Trowlesworthy and Stalldon seem to have a different plan, and are sited at a lower altitude than typical enclosed settlements. But more information is needed before they can be separately classified.

Another unusual enclosure is situated at the Dewerstone, on the promontory which rises 400ft above the meeting of Plym and Meavy. At 725ft above sea level it is the lowest of the Moor's enclosed settlements. It had only one hut, built on the wall. Originally, the wall ran out in a rough U shape from the summit rocks which formed the south-west side, but much of it has disappeared. Probably about an acre was enclosed. No doubt the owners of stock impounded here lived in huts on Wigford Down and only herdsmen remained with the cattle.

The presence of Bronze Age man on the promontory was strikingly confirmed in 1960. A climber (the late Michael

Rabley) discovered a pottery vessel in a rock crevice about 200yd east of the enclosure. It was broken in two but complete except for some decay. When restored (page 36) it was slightly over 5in in height, of squat shape, with two prominent lug handles pierced horizontally, and a flat base. Between the handles was a band of decoration consisting of two shallow lines with a row of shallow circular depressions below. Nothing else like it has come from Dartmoor but it, too, has been dated to main Bronze Age times.

MEAVY AND WALKHAM

North of the Plym, enclosed settlements are more sparsely distributed. One on Raddick Hill (577715), between the Meavy and the Har Tor Brook, is well known for a fortunate find by Robert Burnard when he explored it in 1895–6.

It lies on the north-west side of the hill, in contrast to the southerly slopes usually selected. Why this aspect was chosen is a mystery. The surviving wall describes an arc on the left bank of the Har Tor Brook, 200yd above its junction with the Meavy (Fig 6). Both ends of the wall are 50yd from the stream. Worth considered that the wall originally continued to the stream so that the water formed one boundary. This would have been in contrast to the usual complete enclosure where a stream ran nearby (Erme Pound), and where the wall crossed a stream (near Dendles Wood). At Raddick Hill, mining has disturbed the ground along the stream and its course may have altered since prehistoric times. The likelihood is that the enclosure was originally completed by a wall along the bank or a short distance from it.

The settlement was similar in size to Dean Moor, with ten buildings of 9ft to 17ft diameter and one big hut of 25ft. No sign of human occupation was found in five buildings, but

FIG 6
RADDICK HILL
& HAR TOR
~ Bronze Age Sites

Crown Copyright Reserved.

one of the smaller ones produced pottery fragments—part of a moulded rim with a row of fingernail impressions below, and a fragment without ornamentation, probably from the same vessel. Another hut was paved throughout, and here Burnard made his discovery.

The entrance faced south-west and the hearth lay against the wall opposite the entrance. To the right of the hearth a slab had fallen from the hut wall. When this was lifted a hole was revealed containing a complete vessel which undoubtedly owed its preservation to the fall of the slab. It was $10\frac{1}{2}$in in height, of bucket shape, and had a diameter of 10in at the rim. A substantial rib with lugs encircled it $2\frac{1}{2}$in below the rim, and the space between was decorated with crudely incised chevrons. On being taken out of the hole, the bottom broke into pieces, but it has been restored (page 36). It is similar ware to some of the fragments from Legis Tor and suggests occupation from c 1200 BC.

Fragments of what appear to be a shallow dish, of doubtful date, were found in the large hut. It has been suggested that the hut might have been constructed later than the others. More likely it was the leader's house, contemporary with the rest, as at Dean Moor. It occupied a good site, close to the stream. One hut larger than the others is a feature of many settlements.

The Walkham, also, has one settlement of particular interest, a double enclosure at Yes Tor Bottom (568729) close to the abandoned track of the Princetown–Yelverton railway. It occupies a south slope at 1,200ft and the Yes Tor Brook runs down the hill nearby. To a typical small enclosure of half an acre with two huts, another of two acres with three huts was added. There were four huts close by outside. The settlement was explored by Burnard and the Reverend S. Baring Gould in 1898. Six huts were examined and work on a seventh begun but abandoned owing to 'changes in weather'—the hazard that all workers on the Moor have to face. The finds were the usual charcoal, flint scrapers and flakes, river pebbles and stones, grit rubbers, and small pieces of plain pottery; but two of the external huts yielded significant finds.

The hut nearest the railway track was large, 26ft internal diameter, with walls 4ft thick and an entrance facing south-west. Quantities of tin slag and fragments of glazed pottery were found together near the surface. The pottery was dated to the fourteenth and early-fifteenth centuries, indicating that medieval tinners had used the hut. Below these objects, some fragments of a Bronze Age vessel were dug up. Here was proof of Bronze Age settlers living close to a stream which was to be worked for tin in historic times, and where alluvial tin may well have been present in prehistoric times. (Similar evidence was found in huts at Metherall, investigated in 1934 and 1936 before being submerged in Fernworthy Reservoir.)

In another external hut, with a diameter of 21ft and a south-west entrance through 5ft of wall, the flat base of a pottery vessel was discovered intact. It had a diameter of 11in and had been strengthened by a cruciform rib, an inch wide, on the inside. This method of reinforcing a large base is known elsewhere, but this is the only example to be recovered on Dartmoor. This find, and two fragments from the same hut with fine cord ornament, suggest an occupation date from c 1300 BC.

TAVY AND LYD

Here the enclosed settlements are hard to find. Far up the Lyd there is one (541872) on a shelf 50ft above the river opposite Great Nodden. It is 1,250ft above sea level and the northern-most settlement on the west side of the Moor. It had two huts on the wall and three outside, but they and the wall are much ravaged. The layout can be seen clearly from the side of Great Nodden, which rises like a wall to the west. High ground also shuts in the settlement on the north and east, so that it is sheltered except from the mild south-westerly winds driving up the valley.

The Tavy has four settlements in the area of White Tor. Broadmoor Pound (537785), on the slope west of the tor, has a well defined wall with both lines of facing slabs remaining in places. An area of approximately two acres is enclosed. Six huts are grouped in the higher, northern quarter, and one built against the wall in the south angle. This concentration of the living area is not a pronounced feature elsewhere. Three of the huts were explored in 1898. A fragment of pottery was found, ornamented with a twisted cord pattern of lines and interlocking zigzags. An occupation date from c 1300 BC is probable.

Half a mile to the south, near the fields of Wedlake Farm (540778), lies a larger and unusual group. It was tackled in 1905, one of the early explorations which was disappointing in results and poorly recorded.

The remaining complete enclosure contains two huts, one free-standing and one joined to the wall. There is a pair of semi-detached huts outside the south-east section of wall, one very large (30ft) and the other small. To the south again are ten buildings, described, in 1905, as 'more or less enclosed by rows of stones'. A stream runs through the middle of them to join the Peter Tavy Brook. It seems likely that two more enclosures existed here, one on either side of the stream, of which only vestiges remain. Both would have included part of the stream, and a wall across it can still be seen. It runs from one hut on the west side to another on the east, and then continues down the east bank showing clearly the part of the stream included in the western enclosure.

Apart from the very large hut—which it is tempting to think of as the leader's, with the attached small building as his kitchen—diameters varied between 8ft and 18ft. Entrances faced south and west, and one was paved. Small finds of charcoal, flints, stones and pottery fragments, do not appear to have been preserved and were not recorded in detail. In some buildings the original floor was covered with black, burnt-looking material which was analysed as oxide of iron. The reason for this is obscure but, as a small iron horseshoe was also found 30in down, some use after Bronze Age times is likely. The explorers found the site marshy and wet. Most huts had to be dug to a depth of 3ft before the original floor was reached. In these conditions it was not surprising that so little had survived. Today the site seems better drained, and traces of the unusual layout make it of interest.

DART

The remains of a few enclosed settlements can still be found scattered over the great central basin of the Moor which is drained by the Dart rivers. No doubt these are a remnant of those that once existed. The area attracted development early in historic times and there has been much interference with the prehistoric environment. The medieval 'ancient tenements' were here carved out of the wilderness, and small new-takes continued to be made down to the end of the eighteenth century. Enclosure on a grand scale took place in the nineteenth century. More recently, the Forestry Commission has drastically altered the landscape. In the Postbridge area (East Dart), at least a dozen prehistoric enclosures are known to have disappeared or to have been incorporated in fields and plantations. On the West Dart, which must have been an equally favourable area, comparatively few traces of settlement survive. But it is likely that the prehistoric population of the Dart valleys was not much smaller than that of Avon and Plym where less interference has occurred.

Burnard and Baring Gould explored two of the Dart settlements in 1893. These were the first 'pick and shovel' investigations on the Moor, undertaken to end conjecture about the mysterious 'pounds' and hut foundations.

The enclosures are on the great bare hill of Broad Down, round which the East Dart flows on two sides, a mile or so north of Postbridge. The smaller, known as Broadun Ring, was a settlement of ten huts on a south-east slope, 1,400ft above sea level. Its position high above the river, but below the flat crest of the hill, is similar to that of Riders Rings. The view from it down the river valley is noteworthy.

Examination of a section of the wall showed that it was 6–7ft thick, probably 5ft high, and ruggedly built of blocks of stone without packing. Nine buildings had diameters between 19–22ft and there was one circle of foundations with a diameter of only 6ft, possibly not a dwelling. Four of the buildings were joined together, forming an unusual but much ruined group; no entrances to them or passages between them were found, and the reason for the arrangement is obscure. Some huts had platforms in them, consisting of loose stones rising a foot or two above the floor on well laid foundations. Covered with dry grass and heather, the explorers described them as comfortable beds.

Eight of the buildings were examined but the finds were disappointing: no metal or pottery, only river stones, hearth stones, charcoal, a flint core, and two flint flakes.

The larger enclosure, known as Broadun (636799), is by far the largest on the Moor. It has been much robbed for wall building and the Powder Mill leat cuts through it. Originally

62

it had over forty buildings enclosed in an area of fourteen acres. Ten buildings, with diameters of 9–15ft, were explored. Again the finds were few; charcoal and the usual stones, two flint scrapers, and a piece of clear quartz—perhaps a charm or plaything—no metal or pottery whatsoever. The rewards were inadequate for the enthusiasm and courage of the pioneers.

WEBBURN

In the year following the work at Broad Down, the Dartmoor Exploration Committee, of which Burnard and Baring Gould were members, carried out its first enterprise. Grimspound, one of the larger settlements and already the best known, was selected (Fig 7). Its good state of preservation was due to its particularly solid construction and to the absence of enclosed land and mining works in the immediate vicinity. Stones had fallen from the enclosure and hut walls but had not been taken away for other purposes.

The site had been most carefully chosen. On the western slope of the saddle between Hameldown and Hookney Tors, at an altitude of 1,500ft, the settlement is protected by rising ground on all sides except the west. The wall encloses an area of four acres with the remains of twenty-four buildings. A stream known as Grimslake runs inside the northern wall and tumbles down to join the West Webburn river not far from its source. There are wide views westward from the enclosure over the sombre ridges of central Dartmoor.

The Committee was much concerned with the military possibilities of Grimspound but, in spite of the massive enclosure wall, it is indefensible. The wall had an original width of 9ft in most of its course and an overall height estimated at 5ft. Good slabs of granite had been available in quantity on or close to the site, and the whole wall was constructed of large stones, set on edge or laid in courses. Traces of stock pens remain joined to the inside of the western section.

The entrance is on the south-east side, facing uphill. The

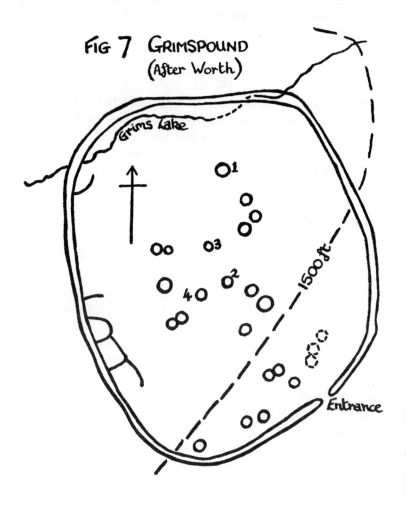

FIG 7 GRIMSPOUND
(After Worth)

Grims Lake

1500 ft

Entrance

Committee cleared away fallen stones and restored it. It is impressive—7ft wide, with 14ft side walls of huge slabs. It was of necessity paved to prevent the passage becoming a quagmire. Today it is stepped, and this may have been its original condition. The pastoral nature of the community is clear, as at Riders Rings and other enclosures, from this wide opening uphill to pastures, and from the remains of stock pens.

How did early man, at Grimspound and elsewhere, manoeuvre large slabs of granite into position? The answer is that two or three men with levers and trigging stones could raise a 10ft slab into a vertical position and, by tilting it at an angle and levering each end alternately, move it over short distances. This method of manhandling the Moor stones has continued in use down to modern times.

The Committee's project at Grimspound was ambitious. From March to June 1894, when weather permitted, they examined eighteen buildings. Five of them, constructed of large stones set on edge and not backed with smaller stones or earth, yielded no trace of human occupation. Hut No 1 in Fig 7 is a good example and has enormous door jambs. The Committee considered that these buildings must have been cattle stalls (with or without a roof), or for storage.

Twelve huts with evidence of occupation varied between 9–15ft in diameter, as at Broadun Ring, and again there was one very small building in addition (No 3 on Fig 7). It had a paved floor strewn with charcoal. No hearth was found, but some domestic use seems likely, perhaps as a communal kitchen.

Entrances to the houses were paved, faced south-west, and had prominent jambs up to 3ft high. Fallen stones on or near the thresholds were thought to be lintels. In two cases a large stone marked the threshold. Two pairs were semi-detached, and several entrances were screened by shelter

walls, as found later at Dean Moor. The hut walls were believed to be 3–4ft high when first erected. Hut No 2 on Fig 7
was restored to show its curved shelter wall, entrance jambs,
and stone-facing of the interior.

Hearths were usually central or opposite the entrance, but
one was to the right of the entrance. Some huts were partly
paved. As at Broadun Ring, several platforms were discovered, occupying segments on the higher side of the huts.
An example can be seen in hut No 4. The early explorers
found no post holes here or elsewhere. No doubt the roofs
were of similar construction to those at Dean Moor. Modern
techniques would probably have revealed at least some post
holes in the larger huts.

Once again the finds were negligible: charcoal, one broken
flint knife, a flint scraper, a polishing stone. In one hut the
cooking hole had been protected by a slab fallen from the
wall, but not even a fragment of pottery was in it, only charcoal and peat ash. In the days before carbon-dating, the
charcoal merely served to show human occupation. None of
the usual water-worn stones were found, probably due to the
distance of Grimspound from a river where they could be
obtained. Lumps of granite had apparently been used in-
stead.

Subsequent to the exploration, a small piece of pottery,
about 2in in diameter, was found adhering to the side of a
cooking hole when it was cleared out more thoroughly. The
fragment was thought to be of similar ware to that found in
other settlements, eg at Raddick Hill.

The dating of Grimspound, in the absence of any metal
or decorated pottery, is difficult. Its isolation from the main
groups, its size and altitude, and the overall quality of its
stones, distinguish it from the majority of enclosed settlements on the Moor. But basically it has the same design and

the same purpose. Occupation during some part of the main Bronze Age seems the reasonable conclusion.

In retrospect, it was a pity that the Committee chose this large settlement for its first venture when they were, as Worth himself was heard to say, 'learning their job'. In spite of the effort and enthusiasm, the enclosure retains many secrets.

In contrast to Grimspound's fame and large design, a small enclosure nearby on the south slope of Hookney Tor (699811) was recorded for the first time in 1958. It is not yet marked on OS maps. The wall is ruined but was originally 4–5ft thick enclosing two huts, one on the wall and one free-standing. Traces of a stock pen remain at the south end. No entrance is visible. This appears to be a typical small settle-ment and it is surprising that no previous record exists. It would be interesting to know whether it had any connection with the large community nearby or whether, as seems likely, it was already abandoned when the larger settlement was flourishing.

At Tunhill Rocks (732758) south-east of Widecombe, are the remains of an enclosure with a single hut. When the site was examined by the Exploration Committee in 1896 it was already ruinous. The rock pile formed one side of the en-closure, as at Dewerstone, and a wall 4ft thick was built out from it. No original entrance to the enclosure was found. The hut had a diameter of 23ft and a south-facing entrance. The explorers were more fortunate here than at several larger settlements. A stone fallen from the hut wall had once again preserved some pottery fragments. Although in poor condition they were sufficient for the shape and general characteristics of a vessel to be hazarded. A fragment of rim with incised grooves forming an imperfect chevron pattern; a piece of a shoulder with a flat cordon and traces of a lifting lug; and part of a flat base—these indicated a vessel similar

67

to the one found in the same year at Raddick Hill. Ornamentation, the coarse and badly fired ware, even the shape, seemed the same. A more recent interpretation suggests that it was perhaps taller and more barrel-shaped than Burnard's pot, but a similar date is likely (c 1200 BC).

CONCLUSION

A small enclosure lies close to the west edge of Fernworthy Forest (647829—South Teign). It had two huts but is now almost wholly obliterated. Traces of seven settlements remain further north in the Taw valley. One, which appears to be a double or even triple enclosure, is on the north-east slope of Steeperton Tor (621891). There are scanty remains of some huts, and a possible entrance in one enclosure wall, uphill and paved in characteristic fashion. The other settlements are in Smallbrook Combe (sq 6290)—fine sites on a south-west slope, protected from the north winds and close to water—and at the foot of the west side of Cosdon Hill (631914/631916). All these northern groups are much ruined and are recorded here simply to show that enclosed settlements existed in the north-east part of the Moor, far away from the main groups.

Skilful siting and the ability to select and manipulate granite slabs of all sizes are obvious; also the great variety of both size and layout. Only one general distinction emerges; some settlements were completely enclosed, irrespective of the number of buildings, eg Tunhill Rocks (one), Broadmoor Pound (seven), Raddick Hill (eleven) and Broadun (forty), others had associated huts outside the enclosures, eg Lyd (two, three outside), Yes Tor Bottom (five, four outside), and Yealm Steps (twenty-one, more than seventeen outside). Apparently some were planned entirely within an enclosure;

elsewhere only herdsmen lived inside with the stock, or perhaps an expanding population moved outside the walls.

In this respect Grippers Hill is particularly interesting, with one enclosure reserved for living quarters; and Wedlake should be noted with its large hut between enclosures, possibly the leader's. All these settlements, however remote, were the homes of families and small communities who had the skills necessary for survival for long periods without destroying their environment.

4
VILLAGES AND FARMS

The open settlements, the villages of predominantly unenclosed huts, are not numerous. Several clusters of up to
ten huts are scattered about the Moor, but only a dozen
groups have sufficient numbers of co-ordinated huts to be
described as villages. Those that can be identified are sited
in the south and west of the Moor, in the same areas as enclosed groups, though generally they lie further up the river
valleys.

Stretches of wall link some of the huts in some villages,
forming enclosures for stock and, probably, plots for cultivation. The buildings did not usually exceed 16–18ft in
diameter but were of similar construction to those in
enclosed settlements. Such evidence as exists suggests that
the villages were contemporary with the enclosed groups, and
like them, mainly pastoral.

There have been no modern excavations, but four sites
were investigated many years ago by the Exploration Committee. The first to be tackled was on Langstone Moor
(557779), Peter Tavy, where some forty huts occupied a south
slope on the right bank of the Walkham. Eleven huts were
explored in 1894–5 and long sections of wall found connecting some of the huts and forming irregularly shaped enclosures. A former watercourse was noted on the west side.

70

Page 71 (above) Typical cairn circle at Belstone; *(below)* part of the unique four-fold circle at Yellowmead

Page 72 Large kists *(above)* at Roundy Park with two coverstones; *(below)* at Merrivale, its massive coverstone split in two by a mason and abandoned

The work was carried out in adverse circumstances—in bad weather, with inexperienced workmen who were continually changing—and the finds were few; a polished red pebble, a flint core and five flint flakes, a scraper and a rubber. In one hut a well defined platform (as at Grimspound and other enclosed settlements) was excavated and there were clear indications of platforms in four more huts. The Committee hoped to renew the exploration another season, but although the site was subsequently surveyed and a plan published, no further work seems to have been attempted.

Today the village sprawls across 400 yards of the gentle slope, a confusion of ruined walls.

In 1896 the Committee investigated a group of forty dwellings and cattle pens north-east of Har Tor, on a western slope above the Meavy (582724—Fig 6). Today less than twenty huts are clearly defined and traces of stock pens are elusive.

Seventeen buildings, with diameters of 10–20ft, were examined. In half of them no evidence of human occupation was found In two huts, circular pits 3ft in diameter and over a foot deep contained much charcoal. One also yielded charred wood, identified as alder, oak and beech. These pits were lined with stones and it seems likely that they had been used for firing pottery, ie a clay vessel would have been placed upside down in the pit and twigs heaped round and over it.

Apart from charcoal and stones, the finds included a whetstone of fine-grained granite, good flint scrapers and a granite rubber. Small fragments of pottery were found in two huts. They were of coarse ware, comparable to the pottery found at Legis Tor and at the nearest enclosed settlement, Raddick Hill. One piece had a thick rim with chevron ornamentation incised below, suggesting that the inhabitants were contemporary with and part of the same culture as the people who made the vessel found by Burnard at Raddick Hill.

The next village to be examined was at Standon Down (551825—page 53), a great bare hill rising from the left bank of the Tavy. The site is on a south-west slope 200ft above the river and between 1,150–1,300ft above sea level. Here the Committee counted the remains of over seventy buildings, in a fair state of preservation, though some walls appeared to have been rebuilt and the huts used in later times. There were traces of connecting walls forming more than a dozen enclosures of irregular shape. The water supply was a spring on the south side of the settlement. Forty-three buildings were examined in June 1901. Many were well paved throughout and nearly all had some paving. Two or three had remains of interior walls forming inner compartments. These, since the excavation at Dean Moor, can be accepted as original features. Charcoal was abundant, suggesting long occupation. Both wood and peat had been used as fuel as in other settlements. The finds of flint were few and unimportant. Pebbles of all sizes, from the Tavy, abounded. The larger ones—the largest measured 20in by 12in by 9in—could have been anvils or pounders. The smallest may have been playthings, but were more likely sling-stones—not for fighting but for use against wild beasts and birds and for controlling flocks (as shepherds in the Middle East still do today). One roughly-shaped stone may have been the upper part of a quern, indicating some cultivation. Small fragments of pottery, found in seven huts, were casually recorded; but in one hut part of a rim survived ornamented with twisted cord, also some plain pieces of the same vessel. This decoration suggests that the village may have been occupied from c 1300 BC.

Four years after Standon the Committee explored the

largest of all the villages, also on the Tavy. Watern Oke (sq 5683) is a phenomenon. The site, far up the river between Western Redlake and the Rattlebrook, is wild and remote. Here the river runs north-west for a short distance, and on the right bank, strung out on a south-west slope, the remains of seventy-four buildings and many low walls are a startling sight (Fig 8). It is a vast jumble of stones and rocks, a man-made extension to the natural clatter which lies between the settlement and the river. A few hundred yards north-east another twenty buildings form an associated group. It is diffi-cult to imagine how so many buildings came to be erected in the wilderness. On all sides the sombre hills shut in the view and this, like Brown Heath on the Erme, is a silent, desolate place where the environment of early man has pro-bably changed remarkably little.

To investigate such a large and remote settlement must have been a daunting task, but the Committee accepted the challenge. In the summer of 1905 they camped near the site, with eight diggers. Twice the tents were blown down, and several work-days were lost through rain. Nevertheless they examined ninety-four buildings. The sheer physical effort is astonishing. Some huts were among rocks, and the explora-tion of them was modestly described as being 'most dis-heartening, and took a great deal of time, patience and strength'. The difficulties throughout must have made the exploration of such accessible places as Grimspound seem a picnic. Interesting features were revealed, but the finds were not commensurate with the effort and many details were recorded inadequately.

The buildings were small, all under 20ft in diameter and only ten exceeded 15ft. They appeared to be rather roughly constructed. Not all were circular; some of the smaller ones being squarish, ovoid, or oblong. These were attached or

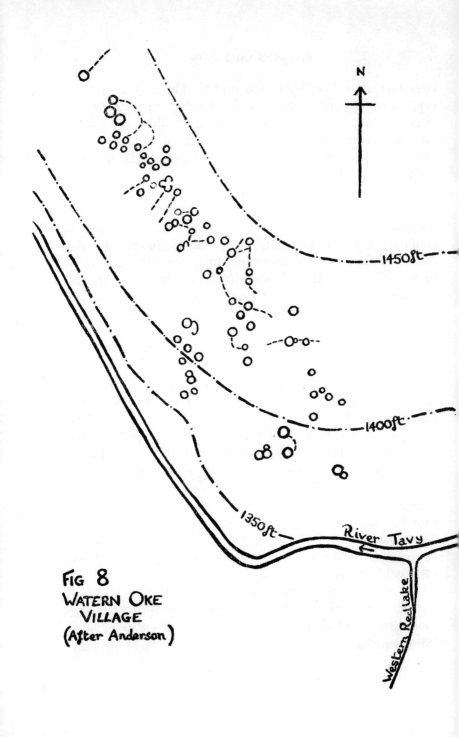

FIG 8
WATERN OKE
VILLAGE
(After Anderson)

close to circular huts and were considered to be kitchens or stores, ie the huts were generally so small that outbuildings had been found necessary. There were two pairs of huts, which seem comparable now to the semi-detacheds at Dean Moor, though of rougher construction. One curious building consisted of three compartments, trefoil in plan, like three half-huts joined together. The entrances mostly faced south and towards the river, but a few faced eastwards. Half a dozen shelter walls had survived, comparable with those found in enclosed settlements. Six huts had paved floors and one a paved entrance. Two huts had internal divisions, as at Standon Down: one was a central wall, the other had boulders cutting off the north-west corner, apparently similar to the arrangement found half a century later in a hut at Dean Moor.

A series of low walls were a feature of the settlement. They connected buildings, or ran from them down to the edge of the impassable clatter, or appear, now, to end for no reason. Cultivation seems unlikely on that rock-strewn slope and the walls must have been for the protection and tending of sheep and cattle.

The explorers were particularly impressed with a cluster of four huts in the main settlement. They were the nearest to the river and only 50ft above it. With a fine view of the river tumbling down to its meeting with the Rattlebrook, the site was the choicest in the village.

Considerable quantities of charcoal were found, far more than in other settlements, suggesting prolonged occupation. Pieces of flint, rubbing and cooking stones were innumerable. A small leaf-shaped arrowhead and two whetstones, one well worn, seem modest pickings from such a large number of buildings. An interesting object was a small glass bead, blue in colour and with a hole bored length-wise through it. Per-

77

sonal ornaments are rare finds on Dartmoor, though of course the bead could be of later date than the village.

Pottery fragments were recovered from twelve huts. Though recorded laconically, some pieces have fortunately been preserved. They show a rare plaited-cord impression as well as twisted-cord and incised decoration. These fragments support the charcoal evidence of long occupation, probably from c 1400 BC.

Apart from the impressive groups at Standon and Watern Oke, the remains of three villages survive in the area of the Tavy. Two are on the Rattlebrook (562842/562846) and the other is in Wedlake Combe (539771), north-west of Roos Tor. The latter consists of nearly forty huts sprawled across the track leading up the combe and in a field of Wedlake Farm. There are traces of paddocks and connecting walls, all much ruined.

Away from the Tavy and Walkham, villages with many huts and connecting walls do not seem to exist, but there are a few open settlements. Twenty-three huts were noted by Worth at Whittenkowle Rocks (585671—Plym) and there is a group of twenty huts near the Swincombe (647723—West Dart). Ten unenclosed huts near Butterbrook Reservoir (645593—Erme) may be the remains of a larger group. Fourteen huts at Lade Hill Bottom (639825—East Dart) were examined by the Exploration Committee in 1898 and yielded a few fragments of pottery.

Two interesting settlements with mixed characteristics can conveniently be mentioned with the villages. They have enclosures with huts and what appear to be paddocks, also fields marked out with lines of stones as at the farms to be described.

At Broadall Lake (611631—Yealm) there are two enclosures, a small paddock, and three roughly rectangular fields all adjoining. With only ten huts, some in the enclosures and some on the field walls, it is rather small to be called a village. But within 200yd across the stream is an open group of twelve huts, built of large stones and with some impressive entrances surviving, which may have been associated with it. On the south-west slopes of Great Mis Tor (sq 5576—Walkham), in the general area of the true villages, there are three dozen huts, some enclosed, some in the open, with remains of enclosures, paddocks and fields.

FARMS

The huts with fields are more numerous than the villages but considerably less numerous than the enclosed settlements. Though a few were recognised earlier, the type has only been defined and studied since World War II, air photography by the RAF during the war assisting the recognition of many sites. A general survey was carried out by Lady Fox, ancillary to her excavations at the largest of them, Kestor.

All except a few are sited between 1,000–1,300ft on the east and south-east parts of the Moor, where soil and weather would have been more suitable for arable farming than elsewhere. The distribution is complementary to that of the enclosed settlements and villages, with a small overlap in the Dart valleys. Occupation of a few sites has been dated by pottery finds to main Bronze Age times (from c 1300 BC) and it is likely that most of them originated then, whatever expansion or alteration took place later.

The fields were marked out by rows of granite stones, some single, some double. No doubt most of the stones were taken from the ground being cleared for cultivation. They could not keep out stock. This was done by herding as can be seen today, eg in Spain, where grazing flocks are driven among unfenced plots of cultivation. Stock would of course have been driven on to the fields after harvest to manure them.

The fields were small, not exceeding half an acre, usually with straight sides, some rather squarish in shape and others oblong. A light wooden plough was used—cross-ploughing has been revealed in similar fields in Cornwall—and lynchets formed on sloping ground. The acreage per hut was small, and the economy was based as much on cattle and sheep as on crops. Droveways between the fields can be seen at some sites. The farm communities were probably even more self-sufficient than those in other types of settlement and except for local excursions to find clay and flint, capable of enduring for long periods without communication with the outside world.

The layout of many original fields has been obscured by use and alteration during the Iron Age and historic times. At Foales Arrishes and Kestor the small squarish fields have clearly been enlarged into long strips, but generally the extent of later interference is difficult to define.

The huts have survived with rather less interference. They are mostly of 25–30ft internal diameter, sited alone, or in twos and threes, at the edge or corners of fields. The average number of huts is about six but only a few farms have more than ten. The larger ones seem to have formed when two or more family groups expanded and linked up their fields.

The huts in a few farms attracted the attention of the Exploration Committee before this type of settlement was distinguished from the others. In 1896 four huts on the east side of Smallacombe Rocks (756782) on Hay Tor Down, were explored. This must have been a typical small farm. It had at least three fields, though the boundary walls are difficult to trace today. The site is important for its pottery finds.

The huts were all substantial, from 22 to 30ft in diameter,

with double walls 3–4½ft thick and at least 4ft high. Large stones formed the inner and outer faces, with small stones and earth packed between. The first hut to be explored produced some flint nodules and flakes, also several fragments of a pottery vessel.

Two fragments are portions of a very thick rim of coarse brown ware. The decoration below the rim consists of three plain horizontal grooves and then a band of cord ornament running like a festoon round the pot. It is a remarkable example of decoration by impressing a twisted cord on the wet clay before firing. Below this are three more plain grooves and then a band of oblique lines also made with a twisted cord. No decoration comparable to the festoon is known from the South West, though a similar pattern incised with a comb has been recorded in Cornwall.

As if this was not sufficient reward, the Committee discovered decorated fragments of pottery in two other huts. One fragment belongs to a vessel similar to the previous find, though the rim and wall are not quite so thick. The rim is unusual, being decorated with three horizontal grooves, and oblique lines are impressed on the neck. Below this again are three more grooves and then a band of interlocking zigzags. All this ornamentation, including the horizontal grooves, was made with a twisted cord. It is the most elaborate decoration found on Dartmoor. The use of the twisted-cord technique suggests an occupation date from c 1300 BC.

Two farms on White Ridge, north of Postbridge, are sited unusually high at 1,500ft above sea level. Together with a similar group of huts, paddocks and fields on Kennon Hill, four and a half miles to the north, they must have been the highest farms on the Moor. The Committee investigated the group on the west slope of White Ridge in 1895 (643818— Fig 9). There are six huts and traces of five fields. The huts

81

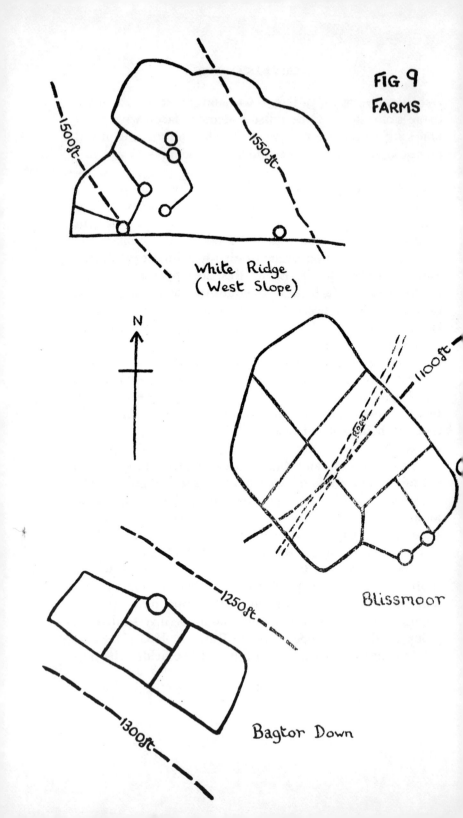

FIG 9
FARMS

1500ft

1550ft

White Ridge
(West Slope)

N

1100ft

1250ft

Blissmoor

1300ft

Bagtor Down

are smaller than was usual in farms—not exceeding 22ft in diameter—and of slighter construction. Good stretches of field walls remain, with lynchetting, and another unusual feature are some curved boundary walls. The site is comparatively remote and has wide views south-west across the East Dart valley to Bellever Tor and beyond. Fragments of coarse pottery found in one hut showed a heavy rim and traces of 'stabbed' chevron decoration, comparable to finds at Legis Tor.

A small farm of particular interest lies on Bagtor Down, south of Saddle Tor (752757—Fig 9). The inhabitants of one hut, standing in its own yard, cultivated three adjoining fields with a total area of slightly over an acre. The site is 1,250ft above sea level on a north-east slope, with a spring rising 20yd below it. The hut had a diameter of 26ft and an entrance facing south-east into the yard. The fields are still well defined, unaltered by later use, and with pronounced lynchetting—negative lynchets at the top and positive lynchets at the lower edge of the slope. It is a remarkably preserved example of a single family group maintaining itself on the Moor.

Another good set of fields is at Blissmoor, north-west of Bowerman's Nose (739806—Fig 9). Even the intrusion of a road has not destroyed the original layout. The inhabitants of three huts cultivated something over two acres divided into six fields. A seventh field was marked out but had not been tilled. They were all squarish in shape, suitable for cross-ploughing, and lynchetted.

At Cullacombe Head, Shapley Common, a small farm of three huts (695824) is situated close to a larger one with ten buildings. Only a hundred yards separates the two groups of fields. These were the first farms to be examined by the Exploration Committee and it was noted that the huts were

83

better constructed than in the settlements (ie enclosed settlements) previously investigated.

Although the modern road across the Common divides the sites, the northern settlement is traceable today. There are three large huts east of the road and eight fields running down the slope and across the road towards the East Bovey stream. The plan is not dissimilar to that at Blissmoor, also now bisected by a road. One of the huts had a special feature: a cupboard in the wall, made of stone slabs, like the wall niche found seventy years later at Dean Moor. Unfortunately this cannot now be seen.

The larger farm has suffered more interference. Use of one hut in historic times was evidenced by finds of a seventeenth-century smoking-pipe and fragments of nineteenth-century pottery—shepherds or herdsmen probably sheltered here. A group of five buildings, joined together in a row at the junction of four fields or paddocks, seems to consist of a house and four outhouses, possibly a separate kitchen (the floor of one small building was thickly covered in charcoal) and storehouses. The living hut was paved and had a platform. Both peat and wood had been used as fuel.

Air photographs confirm a large area of cultivation on Horridge Common in the south-east corner of the Moor. The fields extend on to neighbouring Halshanger Common—where pottery found by the Committee during the exploration of two huts was not preserved—and on to Mountsland Common. Over a dozen huts are associated with this complex, sited between 1,000–1,300ft above sea level. A particular group of four huts (757743) attracted attention recently because of a remarkable find nearby. These four huts have diameters from 18 to 26ft and stand in small enclosures. Around them are fifteen fields with a total area of seven and a half acres, interfered with in later times but still largely identifiable. Some are oblong strips, though much smaller than medieval strips, and some are squarish. Two droveways 14ft wide run between the fields towards water and the open moor.

In 1964 a track was bulldozed through the site, notwithstanding that it was scheduled as an Ancient Monument, in order that timber could be extracted from Bagtor Wood. This instance of Dartmoor practicality resulted in an unexpected bonus. Next year, in the soil disturbed by the bulldozer, a bronze axe head of the type known as a palstave was picked up 60yd from the huts on the edge of an ancient field. It is 5in long, rather worn and corroded, with flanges forming a V. This type is unknown in the South West and is believed to be of Central European origin, imported 1300–1100 BC. Objects have been found in Bronze Age fields elsewhere and the circumstances of the find make it likely that the palstave was dropped when the ground was under cultivation.

Foales Arrishes, near Hemsworthy Gate, was a farm of eight huts which the Exploration Committee tackled in the same year as Smallacombe Rocks. It is sited at 1,300ft on the south-east slope of the ridge between Top Tor and Pil Tor. The original layout is obscured by later use, but three phases of cultivation have been distinguished. The huts and a few contemporary walls adjoining them indicate the area of the Bronze Age farm. Most of the original field boundaries are overlaid by long banks running up the slope to the crest between the Tors. These probably mark medieval strips. Finally, encroaching on the south-east corner of the settlement, are Mr Foale's nineteenth-century newtakes.

The huts vary between 18–30ft in diameter, all double walled, with stone and earth packing, and from 4 to 5ft thick. The largest hut has a special feature. The entrance, though now blocked, faces south-east; to its left a partly paved and curved recess, 13ft long and over 4ft wide, is built out from the hut wall, its entrance at right angles to the hut entrance; in this was found a cooking hole, much charcoal and many pottery fragments, all suggesting that it had been used as a kitchen

The finds at Foales Arrishes included a double-notched scraper, presumably for smoothing arrowshafts. Several single-notched scrapers have been found on Dartmoor but this appears to be the only double one recorded. A fragment of coarse handmade pottery was decorated with two horizontal lines incised below the rim and two bands of small chevrons on the shoulder. This suggests 1200–1000 BC for the first settlers here. Pottery which indicates continued occupation in Iron Age times will be dealt with in Chapter 10.

A large farm at Kestor (sq 6686) provides even more significant links with the Iron Age. It appears to be made up of several smallholdings which, over a long period, expanded and joined together. Its situation near a number of other farms (and the Shovel Down sanctuary) shows that this area was attractive to prehistoric man. The site has been much altered and extended in historic times and the original field walls and huts overlaid or destroyed. Two droveways (as at Horridge Common) are interesting features. It was here in 1951–2 that Lady Fox conducted the first post-World War II excavation on Dartmoor. The results—including the discovery of an iron-smithy—confirmed occupation after Bronze Age times and will be described in Chapter 10. But the earliest fields at Kestor were probably the same as at farms where Bronze Age occupation is evidenced by finds, and it is therefore likely that at least some of them originated in the Bronze Age and were cultivated over a long period.

Other farms on the eastern edge of the Moor are at Shilstone

(Throwleigh) and Buttern Hill, both to the north of Kestor. A large group of fields with nearly a score of huts lies on the slopes of Shovel Down, not far from Kestor, and another farm of six huts a few hundred yards to the west across the Stonetor Brook. Sites at Metherall—mostly submerged now in Fernworthy Reservoir—at Combe Down, Hayne Down and Holwell, show the pattern of settlement. In the Dart valleys fields have been identified on Corndon and Yar Tor Downs and several good examples (with one to seven huts) are on the north-east fringe of Holne Moor, near the Holne–Hexworthy road; and evidence of one farm survives in the Swincombe valley.

POPULATION

The large number of huts surviving on Dartmoor, in all types of settlement and in isolation, raises a tantalising question: what was the population in Bronze Age times?

To try and estimate the number of inhabitants in certain settlements is legitimate. At Grippers Hill, where the huts were all under 20ft diameter, Lady Fox took five to six persons as the number likely to occupy a hut. This gave a community of seventy–eighty provided the herdsmen's huts were permanently occupied. The same rule of thumb applied to similar huts at Legis Tor gives a figure of fifty-five–sixty-five and to rather larger huts at Dean Moor fifty–sixty. Probably up to seven or eight people could live in the large farm huts, so at Blissmoor the inhabitants may have numbered twenty-two and at Smallacombe Rocks thirty. So far so good, but at other settlements additional factors have to be taken into consideration. Some buildings were not apparently intended for habitation—eg at Grimspound, Watern Oke and Cullacombe Head there seem to be separate kitchens, stores and cattle

87

sheds. Nor would all habitable buildings in the larger settlements necessarily be occupied all the time. Conjectures multiply; and an estimate of inhabitants at, for example, Watern Oke, would be little better than a guess.

Certainly no convincing estimate of total population can be given. There are too many possibilities. The settlements were not all in use all the time; and an unknown number have disappeared altogether. With a better climate than today, and a simple but well-based economy, quite a lot of people could have maintained themselves on the Moor over a long period. But it would probably be sensible to think in terms of hundreds rather than thousands at any one time.

Page 89 Characteristic kists at *(above)* Legis Lake and *(below)* Stennen Hill, their coverstones thrown back by plunderers

Page 90 (above) Restored Bell beaker from kist on Chagford Common, decorated with horizontal and oblique lines of incised dots; and restored Necked beaker from a cairn with pit at Fernworthy; *(right)* kist in Archerton Newtake where an archer's wrist-guard was found in 1901. The coverstone has disappeared

5
CAIRNS

Only the graves of important people were marked by cairns, yet more than three hundred burial sites appear on the OS maps of Dartmoor as cairns, tumuli, barrows and kists. Many others have been obliterated in historic times. Those that remain are despoiled and denuded, some only represented by fragmentary hummocks or by a few of the stones that once encircled the burial.

The present-day appearance of cairns is therefore misleading. The circumference may be enlarged naturally in the course of time by overspill of stones and earth, or because the centre has been thrown outward by plunderers. Alternatively, a cairn may be eroded by time and weather, or shrunk by use as a quarry. Measurements should be treated with caution, especially those of larger cairns.

The distribution is not directly associated with any settlements that can be seen today. It seems that most of the cairns belong to early Bronze Age times, ie they were built before the remaining settlements. There is some evidence of later burials, but as the Bronze Age progressed, fewer and fewer cairns were raised. Where settlements were made close to cairns, as at Brown Heath and Drizzlecombe, it was in a period when the older tombs were no longer respected.

Some cairns are on crests, but most were sited on slopes

91

where they can be seen from a distance and where they appear false-crested when approached uphill. This approach seems to have been important and is still marked in many instances by the remains of stone rows. Some cairns appear to be isolated, but most form distinct groups, comparable on a small scale with cemeteries elsewhere in Devon and on the chalk downs of Wessex. But on Dartmoor the cairns were generally simple mounds without berms, ditches or outer banks. There is no evidence that the shallow ditches visible today round circumferences were original. Either turf cutting has denuded the ground, or cattle and sheep have used the cairn stones for rubbing or shelter. The terrain did not lend itself to the construction of the different types of barrow which could be cut and shaped, for example on chalk soil.

But the method of interment beneath the cairn showed considerable variety; and construction ranged from all stone to mainly earth according to the material available. Sometimes cairns rested on the surface, sometimes top-soil was removed or even some of the sub-soil and the cairn built up from a prepared floor. They were not just heaps of earth and stone. Unpillaged ones have been found to be carefully built; for example three investigated by Baring Gould on White Hill (Lydford) in the 1880s. He recorded that two were entirely of stones placed with their smaller ends wedged inwards and one was of earth with a covering of stones similarly arranged.

The typical Dartmoor cairn appears to have been a low mound, rarely exceeding 40ft in diameter, covering a single burial. Much larger cairns exist but nothing is known about them. It has been assumed that they marked the graves of Bronze Age leaders, as in the case of cairns up to 140ft in East Devon, but evidence from Dartmoor is lacking.

It is noticeable that in the area of Avon and Erme the cairns are fewer than elsewhere but are large and crest-sited. The great bare ridges are crowned with man-made 'tors'. Three Barrows on the boundary of Brent and Ugborough Moors consist of a central cairn with a diameter of over 100ft and a cairn on either side of approximately 70ft diameter. They are sited 1,500ft above sea level in a prominent position and are made entirely of stone. In 1872 the northernmost was courageously tackled, before the formation of the Barrow Committee, and with the assistance of some soldiers, by Spence Bate. At least half of it was removed and the soil beneath examined. This laborious shifting of tons of stones yielded no result.

A cairn near the summit rocks on Corndon Down (Dart) is over 80ft in diameter and still over 10ft high. It is founded on natural rock, and whether an interment was intended is not clear. A quarter of a mile to the north is another cairn, over 100ft in diameter. The only records relating to these great heaps are of their spoliation, wantonly and for building-stone.

It would need a major excavation to investigate fully any of the large cairns, and until this is done, and some results obtained, they remain mysterious. The smaller and more typical burial sites must have seemed comparatively easy to explore. Over a hundred of them were examined by the Barrow and Exploration Committees of the Devonshire Association, and by individuals before their formation. Most had already been despoiled and the records are often inadequate; but some finds were made. Particularly important are those that establish the occupation of Dartmoor early in Bronze Age times.

GROUPS

The earliest groups are those where stone rows and kist burial indicate Beaker origin. On Lakehead Hill (sq 6477—near Postbridge) many small cairns were once scattered on the gentle slopes. Modern plantations obscure the cohesion of this group, but at least ten cairns have been recorded at various times within a radius of 600yd of the summit. The pillaged condition of those that can be seen today (Fig 10) suggests that others disappeared altogether when this area was first enclosed. Only slight traces of the cairns remain, but kists and cairn circles in various stages of ruin are sufficient to show what an important area it must have been. All the burials were examined at one time or another and in one the explorers were rewarded. The cairn contained a pillaged kist, the coverstone missing, but in 1898 it seemed that some of the soil inside had not been disturbed. Digging revealed, against one end and overlooked when the kist was plundered, several flint knives and scrapers. They were fine specimens, the scrapers without signs of having been used (page 143). Also in the kist were fragments of pottery. A piece of a rim had an irregular pattern of short incised strokes forming angles and broken lines. It was thought that this pattern had continued all over the vessel. Such flints and pottery in a kist indicate that it was a Beaker burial. Other finds not far away confirm their presence in the East Dart valley.

Less than a mile south-west of Lakehead Hill a similar group lies in Black Newtake (639761–636755–641757) and the adjoining enclosures. Seven small cairns were sited inconspicuously on slightly sloping ground. At least five are known to have covered kists. The diameters of the cairns both here and on Lakehead Hill, where ascertainable, were all less than 25ft. No finds are recorded in Black Newtake but the group suggests the spread of the Beaker people into the West Dart valley. Their presence further south and west in the Plym valley will be referred to when dealing specifically with kists.

Next in date to burials in kists are the cairns, unique on Dartmoor, on Hameldown. This is a linear group spread out along the ridge northwards from Hameldown Beacon. At 1,700ft above sea level they are some of the highest cairns on the Moor. Four of them are marked on OS maps as barrows—Broad Barrow, Single Barrow, Two Barrows—and are important for their construction and for the objects found in one of them.

The size varied, but all had a heap of small stones in the centre, carefully placed, and a ring of similar stones round the perimeter. The rest of the cairn consisted of peaty earth. The burial was found in the area between the stone ring and the central pile, ie eccentrically placed. This was a simple means of making the tomb-robber's task more difficult.

The northernmost of Two Barrows was dug by Spence Bate in 1872. It was then 4½ft high and had a diameter of 40ft. About 15ft in, he found five stone slabs lying on the ground, close together but not overlapping. Under one of these were some cremated bones carefully deposited and the amber pommel of a dagger. In earth taken away from beneath the same stone the blade of a grooved bronze dagger came to light. The point and the base were much corroded but one side was in good condition. Finds of bronze in cairns have been rare on Dartmoor, only a few fragments being recorded, and this dagger and its amber pommel are unique. No handle was found, but if this had been of wood or bone the soil would have destroyed it.

The pile of stones in the centre produced only a fragment of charcoal. This was a token deposit. After cremation, some charcoal from the pyre was placed in the centre and then the ashes of the dead leader were put in the ground a few feet away and covered with a stone slab. Other slabs were arranged to form a paved area by the interment. It is not clear whether cremation took place on the site of the cairn or elsewhere. The cairns on Hameldown, unless one of those on Soussons Common can be interpreted similarly, are the only known examples of this type of burial on Dartmoor.

The dagger pommel (page 54) was cut from a single piece of transparent amber, reddish brown in colour and highly polished on top. It was inlaid with three lines of gold pins forming a cross on the top and continuing down the sides and underneath. Another line of pins ran round the side. In the hollow underneath was a projecting tongue, with two holes in it, for attaching the pommel to the dagger handle. The pommel had been broken before being buried and a detached piece fixed on again with gold pins. The decoration and the repair were of remarkable workmanship. Similar daggers have been found in Wessex and Brittany and dated to early Bronze Age times. Unfortunately the Hameldown dagger was destroyed in an air raid on Plymouth during World War II.

Single Barrow was excavated in the following year and burnt bone, a few fragments of charcoal, and a flint blade with a good cutting edge were found together 6ft from the central pile of stones. One bone was identified as part of a human molar. Nothing was found among the central stones, but the construction and the burial in the south-east quarter of the cairn were identical with those at Two Barrows.

The Hameldown tombs record the arrival on the east edge of the Moor, probably about 1550 BC, of immigrants following in the wake of the Beaker people. Their culture is known for convenience as the Wessex culture. They may have come along the south coast, or direct from the Continent, probably using the Dart valley to gain access to the Moor. A burial found at Kingswear has been attributed to them. They practised cremation, placed rich objects with their dead, and on Dartmoor chose an imposing site for their burials.

Other interesting and contrasted groups cannot be dated with any certainty though they appear to be not earlier than the tombs at Hameldown. Four cairns on Soussons Down (677797), now surrounded by twentieth-century plantations, were investigated by Burnard in 1901–2. They lay close together in a north–south line. The two northernmost were low heaps of stone and nothing was found in them. The other two were mainly of earth construction and are the best examples of this on Dartmoor.

The southernmost had a central depression, indicating previous digging. It stood on sloping ground and the lower side had been strengthened by large stones buried under the earth. A central pit was found in the sub-soil containing charcoal and a flint flake. Further exploration revealed a roughly constructed circle of small stones eccentrically placed. It was 2ft in diameter and contained burnt bone, including a fragment of a human skull, and a flint flake. This seems to indicate similar ritual to that at Hameldown, though the cairn construction was different. Alternatively, there may have been two interments, any bone ash in the central pit having been dispersed by plunderers. But multiple burials on Dartmoor are rare, the only known examples being cairns covering more than one kist.

The adjoining cairn was smaller and had a different type of interment. A central pit contained charcoal and small fragments of burnt bone and there was an area paved with flat stones on one side of the rim of the pit. Charcoal and burnt bone were also found beneath these stones. Above them two pieces of bronze came to light, but as this part of the cairn was riddled with rabbit-holes they may not have been in their original position. They were too small to reveal whether they had been part of a dagger or of some other object. A flint arrowhead was also found. This cairn seems to have covered a single interment of ashes under flat stones, with a pit for charcoal beside it. Again, there may have been some affinity with the Hameldown tombs.

On Holne Moor, near Horn's Cross, five cairns (669712–669707) stretch in a line up the northern slope. The distance from first to last is 500yd and the highest is 100ft above the lowest but still below the top of the ridge. One of them was examined in 1905 and was then 16ft in diameter and 2½ft above ground at centre. A central circular pit with a diameter of 15in contained charcoal and burnt bone. This seems to have been a group of typical low cairns sited on a slope and covering cremated bones in pits—modest tombs compared with any Beaker burial.

On Butterdon Hill, south-east of Harford, five all-stone cairns are prominently sited on the great bare slopes. Two are on the summit (1,200ft). Even allowing for spread of circumference due to interference, they must have been large ones. Down the slopes between 100–200yd away are three smaller cairns which now have diameters of 40–50ft. To the west there are two more on Weatherdon Hill. The importance of this area is further shown by the ruins of several cairns on Western Beacon and on Ugborough Beacon, less than a mile away to the south and north-east respectively. No evidence is available to indicate the dates of any of these. On Butterdon, however, another cairn near the summit seems to be of Beaker origin. Ten stones of the cairn circle remain, all fallen, and from it a single stone row runs northwards, passing in less than a mile a small kist and almost touching the circumference of another cairn. Butterdon was probably a hill site used by the Beaker people and in later times.

CAIRN CIRCLES

Stones encircling burials are often the only indication of the former existence of a cairn and are a distinctive feature of the Moor landscape. They are all found where kist burial is proven, or likely, or where stone rows lead to cairns. They may therefore be attributed to the Beaker people. Examples have already been noted on Brown Heath and on Butterdon Hill. Three of the cairns on Lakehead Hill have well-defined circles (Fig 10), and two in Black Newtake have a few stones remaining. It seems that the stones were usually small and covered by the cairn so that the circumference was outside them; but where the stones were tall, say 4ft or over, they may have stood like sentries on perpetual guard, or at least had their tops above the cairn surface.

Generally, circles were less than 30ft in diameter but larger ones exist. That on Butterdon Hill was 35ft. On Ringmoor Down an even larger one (40ft) was restored in 1909. At that time only one stone remained upright, 30in above ground, and four were fallen. Pits in the ground seemed to indicate where six other stones had stood. The fallen stones were raised, and five tall stones imported from elsewhere. The circle today is therefore only fifty per cent prehistoric, and is not representative. By contrast a small cairn 350yd to the north-west is wholly realistic. A diameter of 11ft is marked by fourteen small stones, four of them fallen. They are of quartz-schorl rock, not granite, and the highest is only 2ft above ground.

Another large circle (50ft) is the remote and comparatively well preserved one on Stall Moor. Twenty-six stones remain, twenty-three substantial and only two fallen. They are irregularly placed, with more on the west side than on the east, which may or may not be an original feature. The average height is about 2½ft, but the tallest is over 5ft above ground. There are still traces of a mound inside the circle, but the shallow ditch outside is not prehistoric. The site is a fine one,

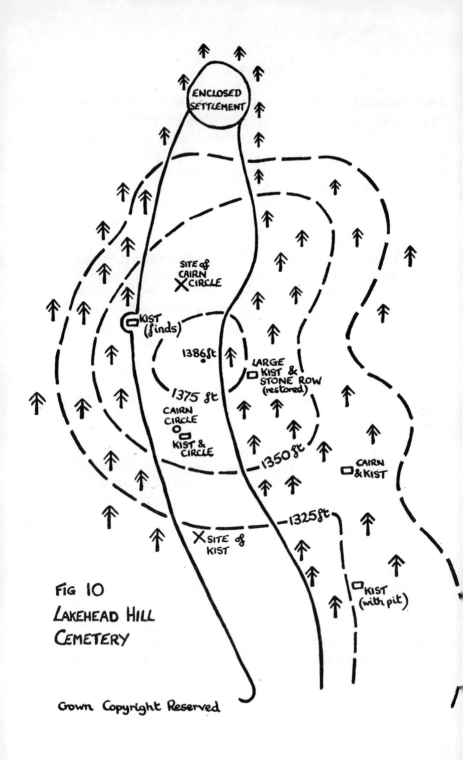

ENCLOSED
SETTLEMENT

SITE of
CAIRN
X CIRCLE

KIST
(finds)

1386 ft

LARGE
KIST &
STONE ROW
(restored)

1375 ft

CAIRN
CIRCLE

KIST &
CIRCLE

1350 ft

CAIRN
& KIST

1325 ft

X SITE of
KIST

FIG 10
LAKEHEAD HILL
CEMETERY

KIST
(with pit)

Crown Copyright Reserved

high up on a bare hill above the Erme, and the cairn is the southern terminal of the longest stone row on the Moor.

The two fallen stones are immediately to the west of the row and appear to be a square slab and a pillar. A similar arrangement is noticeable on Burford Down, also in the Erme valley, where a much smaller circle has contrasted stones—a pillar and a triangular-topped slab—to the west of the row. Such pairs can also be recognised in several rows and must have been carefully selected and placed.

Good examples of smaller circles are those at Trowlesworthy and Soussons Down, and the so-called Nine Stones at Belstone. The diameters range between 22–28ft. At Belstone the cairn has gone, but eleven stones remain standing (page 71). Their broadest sides lie along the circumference and when complete they were probably evenly spaced. Several of them are of the same height, 28–29in above ground, which is unusual. There are also two small stones, inserted in gaps between the stones in the northern part of the circumference, which point towards cairn centre.

Trowlesworthy too has evenly-spaced stones, eight of them, and all substantial. The highest, 4ft 2in above ground, is the nearest on the west side to the double stone row leading to the cairn. The stone row points to the right of the cairn centre, and the tall circle stone, with its broadest side set parallel to the row, points to the centre. Such stones, as at Belstone, must have been deliberately placed. The ritual significance is obscure.

On Soussons Down twenty-two stones remain, more or less evenly spaced if an obvious gap is accepted. They are of varying breadth up to 4ft and the height above ground ranges between 2½in and 4in. All vestige of the cairn is gone, but two sides of a kist remain in the centre.

A few cairns have stones set end-to-end to form a continuous

101

circle. Those round the kist near Hound Tor (741788) are irregular in shape and the circle therefore varies in height and width. Nineteen remaining stones cover two-thirds of the circumference so that the original circle probably had some thirty stones. A continuous circle excavated at Drizzlecombe (592672) was even more carefully constructed, with a uniform height like a kerb. Only one half of it remained.

In a few cases double circles have been found, the inner one close to the burial. Examples can be seen near the Cherry-brook (627787) and on Stalldon (632624). At Yar Tor the inner circle (11ft diameter) was of close-set though not con-tinuous stones, the outer of openly-spaced stones (36ft). The latter has disappeared except for a few stones overgrown with furze and heather. This cairn and the one near the Cherry-brook covered kist burials.

A fourfold circle survives at Yellowmead Down (575678—page 71). No trace of a cairn or burial remained when it was restored in 1921. The fallen stones were uncovered and erected exactly where they lay. One stone only was brought from some distance and erected in the outer circle, so it was an adequate restoration. The innermost circle had a diameter of 20ft and was formed of stones set close together though not touching. Twenty-one remain, leaving spaces for eight or nine more. The broadest is 3ft long and the tallest of a similar height.

The other circles were eccentric, the outermost visibly so. Mean diameters were approximately 38ft, 48ft and 65ft. They were all open circles. The second had the smallest stones, the third rather larger ones (though smaller than those in the innermost circle) and the outermost had the largest of all. They were set so that each circle (other than the innermost) originally had the same number, about forty.

Outside the circles, on the lower side, several stones are

placed pointing inwards. Seven or eight seem to be the remains of a double row leading to the cairn. Next to this row
three more are spaced out like the last stones of a treble row.
Another two may indicate the line of single rows. It could be
that this large Beaker monument, unparalleled on Dartmoor,
originally had several rows leading to it up the slope from
Yellowmead Brook. It must have been a very important tomb
indeed.

CAIRNS WITH PITS

When Beaker influence declined, and cremation became the
general custom, a pit in the soil or sub-soil was apparently the
normal method of interment on Dartmoor. Over thirty have
been found under small cairns, as on Holne Moor, and burnt
bone recorded in nine of them. The failure to find or identify
bone ash is probably not significant as the pits could only be
for cremated ashes.

On Holne Moor the pit was circular. Rectangular and oval
pits and mere shallow depressions have also been recorded,
but some pits were more elaborate (Fig 11).

A cairn in Stannon Bottom was 3ft high when explored in
1896 and was constructed of small stones. The centre had
already been opened but the plunderers had missed a cavity
eccentrically placed towards the north-east part of the circumference. It was shaped like an urn, with a diameter at the top
of 18in, widening downwards and then narrowing again to a
floor of 13in. There was no cover over this pit. Charcoal filled
it and was spread over the floor of the cairn. A few pieces of
burnt bone were identified, also a finely worked flint, probably part of a knife.

In Laughter Tor Newtake three of a group of eight cairns
were examined and found to have pits. One was shaped like a

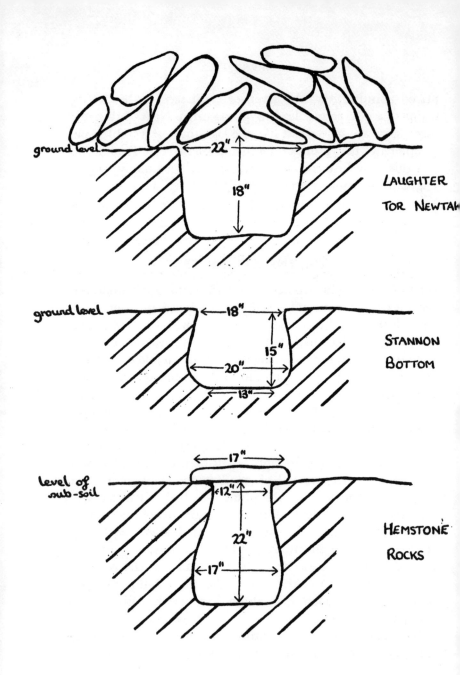

ground level
22"
18"

LAUGHTER
TOR NEWTAK

ground level
18"
15"
20"
13"

STANNON
BOTTOM

17"
12"
22"
17"

level of
sub-soil

HEMSTONE
ROCKS

FIG 11 PITS UNDER CAIRNS
(After Worth.)

bucket with slightly sloping sides. The others were plain round and oval holes. All were protected by cairn stones leaning inwards over them. All yielded a great deal of charcoal, in one case enough to fill a wheelbarrow.

Three cairns north of Hemstone Rocks, now hidden in Fernworthy Forest, were examined in 1900. An urn-shaped pit covered with a slab 2in thick yielded only charcoal; but one of the others had a circular pit with burnt bone and a fired flint. The third cairn had no clearly defined pit, but a depression in the sub-soil contained charcoal.

In the same year the indefatigable Exploration Committee examined nine cairns on Chagford Common. Four had circular pits varying between 8in and 20in in diameter and burnt bone was identified in one of them. Nearby, on Hurston Ridge, a cairn at last yielded an important find.

A central pit in the sub-soil was full of wood charcoal and covered by a flat stone. The inverted rim of a broken vessel was resting on top of the cover. It had been partly protected by a slab leaning over it and held in position by packing stones in the sub-soil. The rim was decorated with horizontal and oblique lines made with twisted cord and in its broken state was removed with difficulty. For many years it was exhibited in Plymouth in the condition in which it was found. In 1960 most of the body and base of the vessel were recovered from inside the rim; and subsequently restoration was carried out from over a hundred delicate pieces. It proved to be a fine urn with a diameter at the rim of 16in and at the base 8in (page 54). The shape and its overhanging rim were characteristic of the main Bronze Age period (1300–1000 BC). The vessel had been inverted over cremated bones, and the pit beneath contained charcoal from the funeral fire.

An apparently different kind of pit altogether had been found in 1872 on the south slope of Pen Beacon. The cairn was about 40ft in diameter originally, though measurement was difficult owing to destruction of the top by plunderers who had thrown stones down the sides. A flat stone covered a pit which was lined with other stones. Fragments of pottery were found with a thick rim tapering to a neck, also an object of soft slate. The latter was oval in shape, $3\frac{1}{2}$in long, and the ends were slightly curved in opposite directions. It was thought to be a tool for modelling clay. Nothing like it has been found elsewhere on Dartmoor.

Page 107 right) Part of the single stone row on Hingston Hill. The largest stones are next to a cairn with a prominent circle; *(below)* the northern section of the fine row on Stalldon

Page 108 Double stone row on Hurston Ridge *(above)* the upper section with a pillar facing a short, broad stone next to the denuded cairn; *(below)* the lower end marked by a substantial stone set across the row

6

KISTS

The small stone burial chambers known as kists are still numerous on the Moor and merit a chapter to themselves. Over a hundred can be found by the energetic. All have been ravaged by many generations of plunderers yet the stones of some are complete. The majority lie in the valleys of the Dart, Plym and Meavy; only a score are recorded elsewhere. Conclusions should be drawn with caution, but the distribution suggests that Beaker occupation was in a broad band north-east–south-west across the Moor. Outside this band penetration appears to have been comparatively slight.

The original Beaker custom was to bury their dead in a crouched position. No bones have been found in any Dartmoor kist. Plundering, and the destructive quality of the soil, could account for this. A kist in Cornwall only 2½ft long contained a skeleton; so those on the Moor, except for a few very small ones, could all have held bodies. Later the Beaker people seem to have practised cremation. Ash also is liable to perish in acid soil, but bone ash was found in kists at Fernworthy and on Langstone Moor. On Lakehead Hill one kist had a pit in its floor containing charcoal, and similar pits in kists have been recorded, eg in the Plym valley, indicating cremation. It therefore seems that the Moor kists were first constructed for inhumations but were still made when the

practice of cremation was adopted. Then, as cremation became general, the building of kists was abandoned and pits,
with or without coverstones, and mere scoops in the soil,
sufficed.

Kists were normally centrally placed in the cairn that
covered them and in most cases ringed by a circle of stones.
Only vestiges of the cairns remain. Some of the circles have
already been described. The burials were almost invariably
sited on the slopes of hills, not the summits. The kists were
constructed of unworked granite slabs, usually with the ends
placed inside the sides, but variations occur. Within suitable
limits the length and width depended on the available slabs.
Pairs of stones of approximately the same length were selected,
and each stone had to have a flat side to face inwards. Height
could be adjusted by digging. Coverstones were any stones of
sufficient size having one flat side to fit over the chamber.
With very few exceptions the length is orientated north-west–
south-east; the significance of this has not been worked out.

There are a few records of stone other than granite being
used. A curious example was noted in 1891 on Great Nodden,
above the Lyd. The hill lies off the granite and the kist was
constructed of the slaty metamorphic rock of the district.
Pieces of slate were piled one on top of the other to form
perpendicular sides and ends. It had been opened and ran-
sacked before 1891 and no trace of it is now visible.

One kist in the Langcombe group (609661) has a side-stone
of quartz rock. On Langstone Moor, east of Whittor (547786),
a kist is made of blocks of the local greenstone. One side, both
ends, and the coverstone remain. It was examined in the early
days of the Exploration Committee without result.

The average size of Dartmoor kists was calculated by
Worth, from seventy-three examples, to be 3ft by 2ft. Depth
could only be ascertained by digging, and the average from

twenty-eight examples was 2½ft. The smallest in the selected group was only 21in long and the largest 4½ft. A few kists, however, were larger than this.

LARGE KISTS

Roundy Park, near Postbridge, is the best known of these (639797—page 72). The internal measurements are 6½ft by 4ft, and when restored the depth was 3ft. The end-stones are single slabs but one side is of two stones, the other of three; and there are two coverstones. It therefore consists of nine stones, unlike any other kist on Dartmoor, and megalithic influence is clear.

One of the kists on Lakehead Hill (Fig 10) is large, 5½ft long, with a coverstone 8ft long and 6ft across at its widest. It was discovered in 1896 under a covering of grey moss. The coverstone had previously been thrown aside, the kist plundered, and then the walls had fallen inwards. It was re-erected, the northern end consisting of two stones outside the side-stones. If one of these stones had been set inside, a kist of normal construction and shorter length would have resulted.

At Merrivale sanctuary a kist 7ft long, with a coverstone 10ft long, had one side made up of two slabs (555747—page 72). Presumably a second slab of 7ft or over was not readily available. This kist also was restored in the last century, but not before a mason had split the fine coverstone in two.

A kist with a single side-stone 7ft long and an end-stone over 4ft was recorded in 1902 approximately 800yd north-east of Wild Tor. The cairn was ruined, but examination of the kist by the Exploration Committee revealed a circular pit containing a little wood charcoal. Two large flat stones nearby were thought to be the coverstones.

The northernmost kist in Black Newtake cemetery (639761)

has a length of 4ft 9in, slightly larger than the largest of the normal kists. It is a particularly fine example, complete except for the coverstone, and not restored. The cairn circle appears to have had a diameter of 24ft.

Worth considered that the restorations at Roundy Park, Lakehead Hill and Merrivale, had been carried out 'too generously'. This may be true, but the coverstone at Merrivale is enormous and the kists near Wild Tor and in Black Newtake were not restored. There is no doubt that kists over $4\frac{1}{2}$ft in length were constructed on Dartmoor. Such dimensions suggest a continuing megalithic influence where the right material was available.

It is difficult to fit the large kists into the chronology of Dartmoor burials. Could they represent a transitional stage between communal burial chambers and single inhumations? Or could they be for bodies laid out at full length, the manner briefly adopted in Wessex c 1600 BC? There is no evidence that this phase of Wessex culture reached Dartmoor; and the pit with charcoal, near Wild Tor, does not support either of these suggestions.

It should be noted that all the large kists (except the isolated one near Wild Tor) lie in areas of considerable Beaker activity. At Lakehead Hill and Black Newtake they seem to form part of Beaker cemeteries. Both were surrounded by cairn circles and a stone row led to the former. The latter differs neither in setting nor construction from normal kists. Roundy Park is also a typical Beaker site and is not far from kists in Archerton grounds and newtake. At Merrivale the large kist is in the middle of the Beaker sanctuary.

It is therefore likely that they were contemporary with Beaker occupation, perhaps constructed for special interments about which nothing is known. The only finds in them— charcoal near Wild Tor, a flint scraper and part of a whetstone at Merrivale—are comparable to finds in normal kists.

SMALL KISTS

A kist with dimensions of 21in by 13in and a depth of 14in was discovered on Langstone Moor at the end of the last century. The bottom was paved, the only known example of this on Dartmoor. The kist was also unusual in that it had not been plundered. After interment had taken place, and before the coverstone was placed in position and the cairn built, it had been filled with sub-soil. In this filling a little wood charcoal and bone ash were identified—evidence of cremation. Later, the kist was removed to Plymouth. However much this may be regretted, its survival on site would have been hazardous.

Another exceptionally small kist, not recorded until 1942, is on Butterdon Hill (658593). The coverstone and one side are missing and there is no trace at all of a cairn. Its measurements are 23in by 15in and the depth about 18in. This is one of the mere half dozen kists known in the Erme valley.

Three kists close together on the north-west slopes of Hingston Hill, in the valley of Newleycombe Lake, were not recorded until 1958 (582694). This is surprising as they lie out in the open and are easily recognisable. One is very small. Owing to an end-stone being missing and the other displaced, the length can only be estimated. It was probably not more than 20in, and the present width is only a foot. It therefore appears to be even smaller than the Butterdon kist and to be the smallest still to be seen on the Moor.

NORMAL KISTS

Excluding the large and the very small, the Dartmoor kists

are a remarkably homogeneous collection. After many years of investigation and recording, Worth cited the Crock of Gold on Royal Hill, near Princetown, as a good example of normal construction (Fig 12). It lies close to the track leading from Tor Royal to Swincombe and its survival is surprising. Traces of the cairn remain, and six stones of a circle with a diameter of 10ft. The coverstone is 4ft square but was thrown aside long ago. The dimensions of the kist are 2½ft by 1½ft, the depth 2ft. Its name commemorates the wishful thinking of its plunderers.

The largest of the normal kists, 4½ft long, is also complete. It is the southern kist of two on Willings Walls Warren (Plym) and was not recorded until 1932. The coverstone is 7½ft long and leans against the outside of the massive northern side-stone. The end-stones have fallen inwards but it is a fine example. Another kist of above average dimensions is near Calveslake Tor (Plym) and there are substantial remains of the cairn. A fine tanged arrowhead was found here when digging was carried out at the beginning of the century.

A kist of average size at Legis Lake (566657) is in good condition (page 89) and the remaining stones of the cairn circle have a diameter of 14ft. The ground is now level with the top of the kist walls, emphasising that it was simply a stone-lined pit. The coverstone has been heaved to one side, as usual, but part of it overhangs the kist. A slightly larger but similar example is the northern kist of two on Stennen Hill (626779, page 89), north of Powder Mills. The coverstone lies along the top of one side-stone, and little imagination is needed to picture an unspoilt tomb. This is one of the few kists with its length orientated slightly north-east–south-west.

A complete chamber, except for damage to one side, is in Joan Ford's Newtake (631722—Swincombe). Here there is a variation in construction (Fig 12). A stone of suitable length

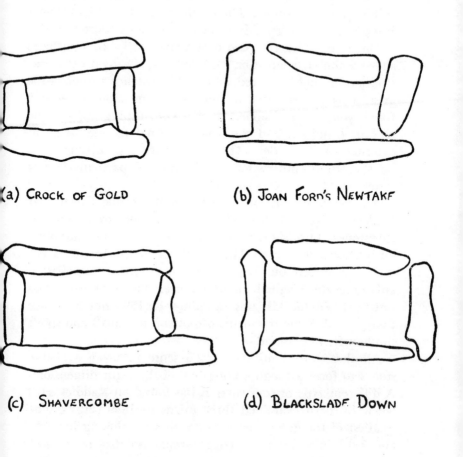

(a) CROCK OF GOLD

(b) JOAN FORD'S NEWTAKE

(c) SHAVERCOMBE

(d) BLACKSLADE DOWN

FIG 12   KIST CONSTRUCTION
(After Worth)

could not apparently be found for the second side-stone, and a shorter slab was used. The result is that the end-stones are internal to the longer side and external to the shorter.

One of five kists recorded near Shavercombe Brook (Plym) shows a similar adaptation (595659—Fig 12). Again the side-stones could not be paired, and in this instance a stone of too great a length was used for one wall. This stone projects a foot beyond one end-stone. Another kist in this group has one end-stone normal and the other internal to one side and external to the other. The coverstones are missing from both of these, otherwise they would be particularly fine examples.

Another variation can be seen on Blackslade Down near Widecombe (734755—Fig 12). Both end-stones are outside the side-stones. This is a tidy kist, the rather thin side-slabs obviously chosen with care. The ruined cairn appears to have a diameter of 40ft but is probably an example of spoliation enlarging the original circumference. The coverstone was nearby when the kist was examined in 1896 but has since disappeared. Some fragments of pottery, too small and spoilt to identify, were found.

All these variations show good sense in using available stones to form a rough oblong box of the right dimensions. A different type of construction was found on Raddick Hill when Burnard examined three cairns in 1899 (Fig 6). The smallest of the group had a kist with sides sloping inwards, and held in position by trigger-stones, so that only small stones were needed to form the cover. A pit under the kist contained wood charcoal. The other cairns covered kists of normal construction. One was complete, the coverstone partially moved to one side and the contents disturbed. However, a small piece of thin, corroded bronze had been left behind by the plunderers—one of the rare finds of bronze on

Dartmoor. The cairns can be traced, but none of the kists are visible today.

A kist near Legis Tor (574654) was investigated at the same time as the enclosed settlement. Only the coverstone and side-stones remain, but the kist had an unusual feature: all the walls originally rested on an earthfast boulder. Apart from the small kist taken from Langstone Moor, this is the only known example of a stone-bottomed kist on Dartmoor.

In 1878 an interesting discovery was made in Thornworthy Newtake (667843—North Teign). A cairn of 30ft diameter covered two kists, both unspoilt. This was the first record of multiple burial. The larger kist, 4in longer than the other, lay practically in the centre of the cairn. The smaller was a few feet away and, because of the natural slope of the ground, at a lower level. They were both orientated north-west–south-east, but with 30° difference.

The central kist was opened and an unspecified flint implement found in it. The smaller kist, with the cover-stone in place, was left for later examination. Unfortunately it was plundered before the explorers could return. The soil thrown out from it yielded flints and some fragments of a pottery vessel, but a great opportunity had been lost. The whole kist was moved eight years later to the Torquay Natural History Museum and re-erected with the cover tipped back to show the interior. The slightly larger kist remains on site, close to the margin of Fernworthy Reservoir. It is still complete, with the coverstone propped against one side-stone, and in good condition.

The pottery fragments from the smaller kist were thin and fragile, but ornamentation by incised lines crossing one another, not at right angles, and at variable distances, was visible; and the base of the vessel was estimated to be 3in in diameter. The record was inadequate, but the size and type

117

of ornamentation are comparable to those of a beaker found subsequently, not far away, at Fernworthy (page 90).

The only other record of multiple burial was in a cairn on the east side of Cosdon Hill. Two kists were found here in 1896, both despoiled and ruined. They were laid end-to-end, but their orientation was slightly different. One stone therefore served as an end for both as can still be seen today.

The good fortune of finding a complete beaker in a kist fell deservedly to Burnard. In April 1897 he noticed a small mound on Chagford Common (676828), 400yd north-east of the fine stone row on Hurston Ridge. This proved to be a denuded cairn, 15ft in diameter, covering a kist of normal dimensions which had not been pillaged.

The kist was found to be full of soil, a thin layer of peaty soil on top, which must have been washed in under the coverstone, and the remainder sub-soil containing fragments of wood charcoal. The soil was compact, as though lightly rammed. When the soil was carefully removed a small vessel was found about 4in above the floor. It lay at an angle in a corner of the kist, its mouth pointing to the corner diagonally opposite. After being lifted and measured it broke up. British Museum staff restored it (page 90). Decorated in bands of horizontal and oblique lines of incised dots, and 10in high, it is of the type known as Bell beakers—the only one to be identified on Dartmoor, and a most important discovery. This type is also found in Wessex and is a derivative of the Bell beakers of the Continent.

Another characteristic Beaker object was found in a kist close to Powder Mills leat, a few hundred yards north of Archerton (637795—page 90). The coverstone was missing, and a pit in the floor had been plundered. But under the eastern side the explorers unearthed an oblong piece of gritty stone about 2in long It had been rubbed perfectly smooth and had a hole at each corner. It was an archer's wrist-guard, to protect the wearer against the blow of the bow-string. The holes were for thongs to bind it to the wrist. It was similar to others found on the Continent and in England (eg at Dorchester near Oxford) but it remains a unique find for Dartmoor.

Apart from the cemeteries at Lakehead Hill and Black Newtake, there are several groups of cairns where all—or the majority—are known to have covered kists. In addition to the Crock of Gold, three kists survive on Royal Hill. Not far away are two kists near Blakey Tor (612736, 613736), and north of the Blackbrook river at Roundhill (sqs 6073–4, 6174) there are the remains of a dozen burials, six in kists. Three of these are close together near the river (605739), forming a compact group like those on Hingston Hill. Royal Hill–Roundhill must have been an important burial area and indicates Beaker presence west of the West Dart, as the Black Newtake group indicates their movement from the East Dart into the West Dart valley.

Penetration continued southwards and westwards, and the Plym (with the Meavy) has as many kists surviving as the Darts. Several of them have already been mentioned. They lie all the way down the river, from Great Gnat's Head near its source to Lee Moor on the left and Wigford Down on the right bank. Fragments of pottery decorated with horizontal incised lines, parts of a beaker, were found in 1900 in a pillaged kist (545645) on the south slope of the latter. The find marks the arrival of the Beaker people on the southwest edge of the Moor. The sides of this kist lean inwards, no doubt from the pressure of the cairn around it, but it was finely constructed and the cairn circle remains.

Further up the Plym a particularly interesting group of tombs still exists in the lonely valley of the Langcombe Brook

119

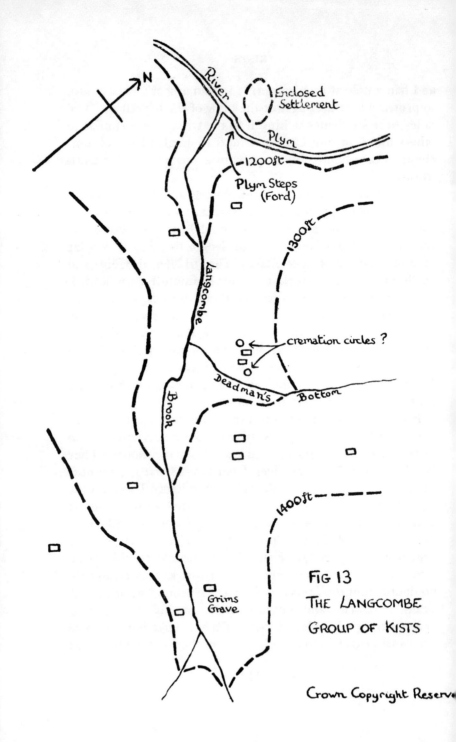

N

River
Plym

Enclosed
Settlement

1200ft

Plym Steps
(Ford)

1300ft

Langcombe

cremation circles ?

Deadman's   Bottom

Brook

1400ft

Grims
Grave

FIG 13
THE LANGCOMBE
GROUP OF KISTS

Crown Copyright Reserve

(Fig. 13). No less than eleven kists lie within 1,250yd of each other on either side of the stream. Three are much overgrown and rather difficult to find, but the rest, in spite of pillage, are good examples. They are all of normal construction except for one which seems to have an end-stone external to the sides, and the one already noted which has a side-stone of quartz rock, not granite. They are all orientated northwest–south-east with the exception of that known as Grims Grave, the greater length of which lies a mere degree east of north.

Five kists are complete, four with the coverstone heaved aside in the usual manner, but one has its coverstone still in position, the only visible example of this. It has been pillaged by forcing side- and end-stones apart at opposite corners. Grims Grave is also complete except that the surviving coverstone covers only part of it, suggesting that there may originally have been two.

Exploration of some of these kists yielded poor results. The kist near Plym Steps, north of the brook, contained only the remains of a fox which had crept in to die not long before the Barrow Committee arrived with their spades. Grims Grave, with its substantial cairn circle, also yielded nothing prehistoric, though a flint flake was picked up a few feet away. But on the west side of Deadman's Bottom—a significant name for the short valley of a feeder stream of the Langcombe—an unusual feature was recorded.

Two kists here are only 30ft apart, one complete though deformed, the other with a side-stone missing and a 6ft coverstone thrown clear. Close to each cairn is a circle of stones of roughly similar diameter. These circles are marked on OS maps as hut circles, but there is no sign of hut walls or entrances. They consist of a single line of stones and resemble cairn circles.

When the one nearest Deadman's Bottom was examined by the Barrow Committee it was found to be paved with flat stones laid on the sub-soil of decomposed granite which, in this area, is umber-coloured. A little charcoal was recovered from between the paving stones, and beneath them the sub-soil was light redbrick in colour, changing to natural colour a few inches down. The red colour went deepest in the centre of the circle. It seems that considerable fires had once been maintained on the paved floor.

The other circle was similar in construction but the pavement was laid on top-soil which had protected the sub-soil from any heat. The suggestion is that these may have been cremation sites, used for a series of cremations. Their rather central position in the Langcombe group, and the fact that five kists are visible from them, may be of significance. Although another floor was recorded, not far way by a kist on Great Gnats Head, it is strange that nothing similar has so far been identified elsewhere on Dartmoor.

The complete kist near Deadman's Bottom was also explored, but without result. Its neighbour, the nearer to the stream, rewarded the men who had carried their tools so far into the Moor. A foot or so of peat was removed from the kist and pottery fragments were found resting on and partly embedded in the sub-soil floor. Small pieces of rim, wall, and base were well enough preserved to indicate a beaker 7in in height, ornamented with horizontal incised lines. This was not all: where the side-stone had been removed, three unused arrowheads had been overlooked, or ignored, by previous diggers. They were of fine workmanship, tanged and with short barbs.

7

ROWS, CIRCLES, AND STANDING STONES

William Crossing described these monuments as unimposing and pointed out that, in some cases, larger stones available not far away had not been utilised. But, he added, the visitor would certainly 'not fail to be pleased with his surroundings'. All this is true. The monuments are insignificant in the vast landscape of the Moor—the stones of the rows and circles mainly small. Yet the persistence of a wild and remote setting should not obscure the intrinsic interest of these expressions of early man's aspirations. With few exceptions, construction was consistent, and presumably the Beaker people, and possibly the inheritors of their traditions, knew what they were doing. They did not work or import stone. Selection of local material alone produced the Dartmoor monuments.

The rows have been attributed to the Beaker people because of their analogy with the great stone avenues in Wessex. Though no Beaker object has so far been recorded in a cairn sited at the end of a surviving row (a typical Dartmoor inconclusiveness), three cairns with kists have rows leading to them—a triple row to the double burial on Cosdon Hill and single rows to the large kist on Lakehead Hill and to one of the kists on Roundhill. The triple row at Yar Tor, though the upper section has disappeared, is in line with and undoubtedly led up to a recorded kist. On Brown Heath, also, a kist was recorded in the cairn at the head of the double row. These kists were Beaker burials. However, it may be that later immigrants were responsible for some of the rows, ie a few may have led to cairns without kists. That they were all erected in early Bronze Age times is generally accepted, though the only one to be excavated (Cholwich Town 1961) yielded no evidence as to date.

The stone circles are also attributed to the Beaker people, not only because of similar monuments in Wessex (especially Avebury), but because their distribution, with one or two exceptions, coincides fairly well with areas where there is evidence of Beaker occupation. Their use as important ceremonial sites, perhaps even their construction, may have continued well into Bronze Age times. At Fernworthy and Merrivale they form part of the Beaker sanctuaries, but it may be significant that the others are not so closely associated with stone rows and known Beaker burials.

The few identifiable standing stones are clearly of the same culture as the large stones at the ends of rows and in circles.

ROWS

Consisting of single, double and triple lines of stones, over sixty were recorded by Worth and his father R. N. Worth. Some of these are now mere remnants, difficult to recognise, and one or two have disappeared altogether during the last eighty years. One or two were not included in the list and others have been recorded since 1950. Over sixty can, therefore, still be traced, forming a collection as unique as the Moor kists. More than half lie in the valleys of the Teigns, Darts, Plym and Meavy. But the distribution differs from

125 (above) Unrestored
cle at Scorhill, with twenty-
ee stones still standing— the
t example of this type of
nument on the Moor;
ght) the impressive Stand-
Stone known as Beardown
n, rising eleven and a half
t out of the ground

Page 126 (
The Long-
stone on
Shovel Do
once mark
the end of
two stone
rows

(right) The tallest of the
terminal stones at Drizzlecombe, re-erected in 1893,
and standing fourteen feet
above ground

that of kists in one important respect: good, indeed unique, examples of rows are to be found in the valleys of Erme and Glazebrook where kists are comparatively scarce. This may suggest that some rows were built after Beaker influence had declined.

Normally, rows led to cairns and had a tall stone, the so-called blocking stone, set transversely at the other end. Where both ends are not defined the original length is a matter of conjecture. Many rows have been robbed, the smaller stones not difficult to remove, and tempting to wall and road builders; the larger stones in demand for gate posts. Definite lengths range from 35yd to over two miles. The longer rows are all of single lines of stones.

Unlike kists, the rows have no particular orientation. Their direction seems to be governed entirely by the lie of the ground. A gentle slope was chosen wherever possible, and the cairn erected generally at the higher end so that it appeared false crested when approached along the row. Some rows point to cairn centres, some are aligned off-centre, usually to the right. There are also rows which touch cairn perimeters or pass close to them. There is one example, at Merrivale, of a cairn set in the middle of a row.

Characteristic examples of single and double rows can be seen on Hingston Hill and Hurston Ridge respectively. The latter, a mile north of Warren House Inn, is one of the best preserved of all the rows on Dartmoor (page 108). It consists of nearly fifty pairs of stones laid out on a gentle slope with a cairn at the higher end. The length is about 150yd, the stones being irregularly spaced but not exceedingly so; and the distance between the two lines varies. A pronounced widening, as the now denuded cairn is approached, seems intentional. The stone next to the cairn in the eastern line is the largest in the row, a fine pillar nearly 6ft tall. The western terminal stone facing it is a low, broad slab, the pair possibly being male and female symbols. Other pairs in the row, though of smaller stones, show similar shapes. The lower end is marked by a slab nearly 5ft high set across the row. It is considerably bigger and taller than any of the other stones except the large one next to the cairn.

The characteristic features are: the long axis of stones in line with the row; a cairn at the higher end with a large transverse stone marking the lower end; varying width between the lines and irregular spacing of stones; and the largest stone next to the cairn paired with a smaller one.

The row on Hingston Hill (sq 5869—page 107) has similar characteristics so far as they are applicable to a single row. About 160 stones, irregularly spaced and some now fallen, cover a distance of about 340yd. The lower end is marked by a stone standing some 5ft above ground and set with its axis across the row. From this stone the row descends slightly for a short distance, then levels out, and then climbs to what must have been an impressive cairn—the remaining circle of twenty-six stones has a diameter of 37ft. Spaced irregularly along the row are stones of above average size, and as the cairn is approached they become alternate. Finally, there are three large stones next to each other, increasing in height towards the cairn, the nearest to the cairn being a splendid pillar over 9ft above ground. The row does not run in an exact straight line from end to end, but curves slightly towards the north.

Both of these typical rows give the impression that their builders, though selecting and positioning certain stones with care, were not seeking geometrical accuracy.

A single row on Stalldon between Erme and Yealm (sq 6362 —page 107) consists of much larger stones than usual. They are widely spaced and the row is a long one, covering nearly

550yd, and slightly curved. The stones increase in size towards the northern and higher end, where four of them are between 6ft and 8ft in height. They reach to the crest, an unusual feature, and can be seen on the skyline from considerable distances. Apart from its curve, and having the largest stones at the higher end, this row bears no resemblance to any other row on Dartmoor. The stones are so much bigger overall and there is no cairn at the higher end nor tall terminal at the lower. At one point the row touches the edge of a cairn, and there are two cairns close to it, one on either side. Their relationship to the row is not clear and they may be of later date. Although the ends of the row are not defined, there is no evidence that it was originally longer. The significance of it, the ceremonies associated with it, seem even more mysterious than those of the characteristic rows leading direct to burials. The long line of big slabs climbing the slope is visually more impressive than any other row on Dartmoor and constitutes a sombre, puzzling monument.

On the north-east slope of Glasscombe Ball (661608), in the valley of the West Glaze, lies another row of special interest. It is nearly 200yd long, and approximately three-fifths of it (the higher part) is a double line of stones, the remaining two-fifths a single line. Traces of cairns were found at both ends. The single row is formed by prolongation of the western line of the double row and there is no surface evidence that it was ever double. Possibly the double row was erected first, leading up to a cairn in the normal way, and the lower cairn and single row added later. The specific significance is obscure.

Another example which may have had a cairn at the lower end is the most prominent double row near Laughter Tor. Many of the stones are missing, having no doubt been used in the construction of the newtake wall which cuts through the row. Those that remain form two small groups, one of eight stones north, and one of ten stones south of the wall. The northern and higher end is marked by a fine tall stone. This was fallen, when identified, and was re-erected to stand over 8ft above ground. The stones at the lower end have a greater width between them than the other group, and the two largest stones are at the lower end. These features indicate that a cairn may have been sited at the lower end, though no trace of it remains. It may be relevant that other cairns recorded in this area have disappeared, and remnants of other rows and many set stones in the area may be the remains of a complex comparable to the sanctuaries to be described in Chapter 8.

The steepest row is at Assycombe (661826), among the oppressive plantations of Fernworthy Forest. A double row climbs up 60ft in a length of 140yd. The slope is slightly convex overall so that the cairn cannot be seen from the lower end, only the top of a large stone next to it is visible. The cairn would therefore have come gradually into view as the row was ascended, an unusual arrangement.

A slab about 4ft high is placed across one of the lines of stones to mark the lower end. Nearly seventy pairs of stones and several single ones remain: less than a score appear to be missing. Some pairs consist of small broad stones facing pillars. The lines are typically irregular as they mount the hillside. Most of the stones are small, but two pairs of large stones were placed next to the cairn. A big slab over 6ft high, which now appears to be part of the cairn circle, blocks the end of the row. It has been re-erected, perhaps not in its original position; and as two of the large stones at the top of the row have fallen, and another is leaning, the layout is confused. Although on a very steep slope, Assycombe must have been a characteristic double row.

In contrast, a single row on Langstone Moor (550788) is laid out on almost level ground. It was found by Baring Gould in 1893 and was originally about 110yd long, a tall stone marking the southern end and a cairn the northern. The stones were of local igneous rock, not granite. Today, the cairn is barely discernible, and less than a score of the small stones remain. The terminal-stone, however, was a fine one. It had fallen before Baring Gould examined the row, but was re-erected by order of the Duke of Bedford and stands over 9ft above ground. Unfortunately it was used during World War II as a target by soldiers training on the Moor, and the marks of machine gun bullets are visible on it.

Triple rows are comparatively rare. Those at Yar Tor and on Holne Moor (675709) have been much robbed, and one recorded at Red Barrows has disappeared altogether. On Cosdon Hill the restored lines, though cut by a peat track, are well defined for about two-thirds of their remaining length. The site is a nearly-level piece of ground on the east side of the great hill, but the escarpment rises steeply above the cairn at the higher end. This cairn contains the double kist already described. All these triple rows must have led to particularly important burials. The best surviving example is on Challacombe Down, even though the lower end has been entirely destroyed by mining operations.

The present length is about 170yd; how much has been lost cannot be exactly determined, but judging from the lie of the ground it is unlikely that it ever exceeded 200yd in length. The southern and higher end is marked by a very large triangular-shaped slab placed transversely across the lines of stones which narrow towards it. If a cairn was ever associated with the rows it must therefore have been at the lower end, as at Laughter Tor. The rows are well defined. A transverse slab across the present lower end was placed in position when

131

the row was restored. Neither this, nor the small circle of stones visible west of the rows, has any prehistoric significance. The stones forming the latter are probably some which were dumped there when the lower ends of the rows were cleared; the restorers set them up where they found them.

At over 1,400ft above sea level Challacombe and Cosdon are two of the loftiest rows on Dartmoor. Other rows at about the same altitude are the fine double rows on Hurston Ridge and at Assycombe, and the remnant on Langstone Moor. The only rows that reach a higher elevation are a long row in the Erme valley, and the remains of double rows on White Ridge (East Dart) and Conies Down (Cowsic). The latter is the highest recorded row, reaching over 1,600ft at its northern end. It is much ruined, and there is no sign of a cairn, though Crossing wrote that 'not far from the southern end appears to be the remains of a small cairn'. A recumbent pillar 9ft long at the higher end is likely to have been a terminal-stone. It may be that this row resembled that at Laughter Tor.

Pairs of rows have been recorded. Two cairns near Collard Tor, Wotter, about 6yd apart, are approached by single rows which have been much disturbed. The rows diverge by 5½°. This is the pattern with associated rows, more strikingly shown at Trowlesworthy near the head of the Blackabrook. There, the cairns are over a hundred yards apart, and the rows diverge by 70°; but as both rows are aligned on the eastern cairn there is little doubt about their association. The row to the eastern cairn—which has the fine circle of eight stones already described—is double. It starts near the Blacka-brook and runs up the slope with a slight curve towards the east. The Lee Moor leat cuts through it and some of the lower section has probably disappeared, but more than a hundred stones remain, mostly in pairs. Originally, it was as typical a row as that on Hurston Ridge and was of similar length.

The western row, situated entirely below the leat, is today a single line of stones. It starts at a tall stone, and then thirty-eight stones, with considerable gaps, run up the slope to a ruined cairn with traces of a circle. The line of the row, projected beyond the cairn, leads directly to the cairn at the head of the eastern row.

Samuel Rowe in his *Perambulation of Dartmoor* (1848) referred to the western row as double; and in 1871 Spence Bate described it as having sixty stones in its northern line and forty-two in the southern. By 1892 R. N. Worth recorded the single row that can be seen today. Destruction must therefore have taken place about a hundred years ago. It is odd that one line should have disappeared when so much of the other remains; but the position of the terminal slab at the lower end, off-set from the surviving row, is consistent with the former existence of another line of stones.

A pair of rows at Har Tor, in the angle between the Meavy and the Har Tor Brook (Fig 6), has also been partly destroyed. The cairns are only a few feet apart, the rows both aligned north-east–south-west but diverging by 18°. A mining gully has been cut through them. The southern row is single, with only four stones remaining above the gully, and ten below. The northern is double and of great interest. Though now starting some 10yd from the left bank of the Meavy it has no formal terminal and may originally have started closer to the river. Over forty pairs of stones remain, in spite of mining activity in this area, and the typical irregular course and spacing of stones can be well seen from the slopes of Black Tor across the river. Some of the pairs in the row seem to be pillars facing broad stones, and the pair next to the cairn is a smaller version of the fine pair at Hurston Ridge. The pillar stone, however, lies on its side and the broad stone opposite is much weathered. The cairn has a circle of fourteen stones.

Several groups of more than two rows have also survived. One astride the East Glaze, near Corringdon Ball Gate, is unimpressive to look at but has a remarkable layout: a double row east of the stream and a single and two triple rows to the west. The double row was only identified in 1945, and not until the following year was a proper survey of the group made by Worth.

The row east of the stream has been cut by two leats and considerably despoiled. Some forty stones remain, only a few in pairs, but they are sufficient to show irregular spacing, an increasing width towards the cairn at the eastern and higher end, and a small deviation in direction. In other words, it was once a typical double row, though the one-in-ten slope is steeper than usual. The largest stone surviving is less than 3ft high. The row begins 25yd from the stream, but as at Har Tor there is no formal terminal and it may have started nearer.

About 100yd west of the stream and in line with the double row is a small cairn. A single row leads to it from the west, its alignment diverging a few degrees from that of the double row across the stream. The biggest of the dozen or so stones remaining in this single row is a mere two feet above ground.

A few yards south-east of the small cairn is another cairn with a diameter of 37ft and the remains of a circle. Two triple rows, diverging a few degrees from the single row and from each other, lead to this larger cairn. They have been robbed extensively and the remaining stones are mostly less than a foot above ground—none exceed 2ft. The whole complex is insignificant yet tantalising. Who were the important dead whose tombs merited this multiplicity of rows? Other groups of rows form part of the sanctuaries to be described in Chapter 8.

Three single rows in the Erme valley are exceptional, varying in length from 550yd to over two miles. The shortest is therefore only equalled by the row of large stones on Stalldon, the higher end of which lies in the Erme watershed. Apart from their length, these rows have similar characteristics to other single rows. They do not seem to represent a new idea, rather an idea carried to excess. Perhaps the spacious slopes of the Erme valley inspired them. Perhaps they are of later date than the normal Beaker rows, an attempt by a new generation to exceed the achievements of their ancestors.

The least is on Burford Down, half a mile north of Harford. The row starts on practically level ground and then, after being cut by a newtake wall, mounts the gentle slope to a cairn 300yd west of Tristis Rock. A large fallen stone lies next to the cairn. The row petered out at the newtake wall, 400yd down the slope from the cairn, and consisted of some seventy stones. In 1953 a careful examination by Hamlyn Parsons traced the row for 150yd beyond the wall, its alignment curving slightly westwards. This made it about as long as the Stalldon row though the stones are all much smaller.

The lower end was originally marked by a tall stone, now cut in two. The base is 4ft wide and rises over 2ft out of the ground at an angle, so that the stone was leaning when cut. Presumably this was done by a mason in search of a gate post who then abandoned it, leaving a slab over 7ft long and tapering to a breadth of 2½ft lying on the ground. It must once have been an impressive terminal, comparable to those at Laughter Tor and on Langstone Moor.

The row running from Piles Hill to Butterdon Hill was nearly 1¼ miles in length. A fallen stone 8½ft long marks the

135

northern end on Piles Hill. From here the row descends for about a third of its course, then climbs to the cairn circle near the summit of Butterdon Hill already described. An unusual feature is that this cairn is sited 70ft below the other end of the row.

As in the case of the Burford Down row, the length was not known to recent explorers until 1940. The northern section was destroyed in 1803 and only the discovery of an earlier map during World War II enabled the fallen terminal on Piles Hill to be identified and the original length ascertained. Other sections of the row have been confused by its adoption as the boundary between Harford and Ugborough Moors and the introduction of modern boundary-stones. It was also cut by the Redlake Mine Railway, early in this century. But the original stones of the southern section are typically small and irregularly spaced, and the row has a slight curve westwards. About four hundred stones remain out of at least two thousand. Only a well-organised community could have selected and set them up. It is unfortunate that this monument has been so disturbed in spite of its lofty position.

The longest of the long rows, from Stall Moor to Green Hill, is as much a phenomenon as the village at Watern Oke. Who conceived this monument, stretching more than two miles over hilly country and crossing two rivers? What was its special purpose? Several suggestions have been made—for example that it marked a tribal boundary or a processional way, or that it played some part in funeral games. Certainly it seems to have linked two important burials, far apart and separated by terrain different from the setting of any other alignment. More than this cannot at present be said.

The southern end is marked by the great cairn circle on Stall Moor. From here the line of stones, with many small changes in direction due to the undulations of the ground, approaches the Erme, crosses it and its tributary Redlake, and goes on up the slope of Green Hill to a cairn 1,500ft above sea level. During its course the row rises over 300ft. It is probably the longest prehistoric stone row in the world.

The stones are generally small, the only stones available in sufficient quantity on this part of the Moor. In 1892 R. N. Worth counted nearly eight hundred of them, probably a mere quarter of the original number.

In several places south of the Erme the stones have become buried under peat deposits. Analysis of the peat by I. G. Simmons suggests that it was formed in open country with some hazel, oak, and alder thickets in damp places. Peat is believed to have formed at this height after early Bronze Age times. The analysis cannot date the row, but at least it does nothing to alter the view that the Dartmoor rows originated then.

The excavation of a single row at Cholwich Town (584622) in 1961, by George Eogan, generally confirmed previous conclusions. The row was 235yd long with at least ninety-one stones originally, leading to a cairn at the higher end with a circle of eight stones. Fifty-three stones remained standing in the row, and six round the cairn. All were of undressed granite set from 6in to 2ft in the ground, some packed with small stones. The terminal at the lower end, beyond which no sockets were traced, was 3ft above ground. All stones had their long sides in line with the row and the spacing was mostly irregular. Towards the cairn, however, the surviving stones were evenly matched in spacing and in height above ground, and carefully erected, eg two had pointed ends downwards so that the tops were flat. The largest stone, 4ft above ground, was near the centre of the row; but the stone nearest to the cairn was missing and it may have been larger.

This was a typical single row, but one interesting fact emerged. Soil pollen analysis indicated that it had been built in a clearing. This is no guide to dating because it is not known whether the clearing was made by the builders, or by earlier settlers. Nor should this finding necessarily be applied to other Dartmoor rows. At 800ft above sea level the Cholwich Town row was one of only nine recorded below 1,000ft, all lying on the fringe of the Moor between the Lud Brook and the Meavy. The higher sites, as at Stall Moor, are unlikely to have been covered entirely by trees or scrub, especially those well above the valley bottoms.

CIRCLES

Twelve of these are known, widely scattered over the Moor, though none are recorded in the south-east. They are all sited over 1,000ft above sea level, except for one at Brisworthy, the south-westernmost, which lies at 875ft. Diameters range from 60ft, comparable to large cairn circles, to 116ft. Rough and ready in construction compared with the noble circles of Wessex, a common derivation from Neolithic henges is clear, though the surface of Dartmoor discouraged the making of ditches or earth banks. Cairns are often sited near them, and at Merrivale and Fernworthy (Chapter 8) they form part of groups of burials. A sepulchral association is evident, but they may have been the scene of other ceremonies.

All sizes of stone were used and generally they were placed irregularly round the circumference. No attempt seems to have been made to form perfect circles, though this could have been done by fixing a central point and using a cord to mark out the circumference.

The circle near Sowton Tors (547896) is a large one (110ft

diameter), but its score of surviving stones are all fallen. At Down Ridge, near Hexworthy, destruction is even more apparent: only four stones are standing, and three fallen, making a negligible monument. A field wall nearby probably explains its destruction. Similar robbery is evident at Sherberton, on the hills between the West Dart and the Swincombe. The circle has nine stones erect and two fallen; the latter are big slabs which would have stood over 5ft above ground. With a diameter of nearly 100ft the circle has lost a great number of stones—no doubt to the stone hedge which cuts the south-west arc. The site is most carefully chosen, but the fine views cannot compensate for its destruction.

On Langstone Moor a circle with a diameter of 60ft is also now in sorry condition. It was re-erected towards the end of last century, and was subsequently described as 'perfect'. Sixteen stones were standing and there were three other stones outside the circle. There is no evidence that these formed part of a second, concentric circle, and their significance is not known.

During World War II this monument was wrecked by troops training on the Moor. Today only six stones stand to their full height. Four are fallen and broken; six are sad-looking stumps, their tops deliberately knocked off and lying on the ground nearby. One substantial stone outside the circle remains a mystery. The magnificent site, 1,450ft up, can still be appreciated. The ground rises gently to the north and west so that the circle was not on a crest but stood against the sky when approached from the south. The Langstone row, with its tall terminal, is half a mile away north-west; and two cairns lie 100yd south-east, three more some 500yd south-west. The circle may have been an integral part of an important burial and ceremonial area, though more dispersed than at recognisable sanctuaries such as Merrivale.

White Moor Circle (633896), on the saddle between White Hill and Little Hound Tor (on OS maps marked Hound Tor), was restored by the Exploration Committee a few years after the Langstone circle. It was then described as 'inferior in size and dignity', but the reverse is now true. With a similar diameter (66ft) it cannot ever have been the least in size, and if its stones were smaller, they are better preserved. In spite of the action of turf cutters skimming the surface, of rain and cattle breaking up the exposed soil, of cattle using the stones for rubbing off winter coats, of masons in search of suitable stone to fulfil their commissions—in spite of centuries of deliberate damage and fair wear and tear, the remains of eighteen stones out of an original nineteen survived for the Committee to re-erect. One stone had its top broken off and three were represented by their tops, the lower parts having been taken away. The rest were in reasonable condition considering nearly four thousand years of exposure. The position of the missing stone was marked by a pit and by chippings struck from it before removal. Another gap in the circle was apparent, but digging down to the sub-soil revealed no trace of a stone hole. This may, therefore, have been an original entrance, at approximately the northern point of the circumference.

The circle is crest-sited when approached from east or west. The blocks of stone, alone on the bare ridge, are impressive against the sky. But to north and south-west the ground rises gently and the expanse of the Moor dwarfs the stones. Ceremonies at the circle could have been watched from these slopes by any number of people without disturbing the solemnity of the rituals.

Seventeen stones stand to-day, the two tallest about 4½ft above ground, one a pillar and the other a broad slab. The stones are predominantly broad, but there are three distinct

140

pillars, and facing each of them, on the opposite side of the circle, is a broad slab. This appears to be comparable to the pairing of stones in many double rows. A cairn lies close to the circle, and 170yd to the south-east is the standing stone known as White Moor stone. No site on Dartmoor is more mysterious and evocative.

The circle at Brisworthy (Plym), though of larger dimensions, can never have been so impressive as those on Langstone and White Moors. When surveyed in 1909 it had a diameter of 88ft, and four stones standing, eighteen fallen. Sites for three more were evidenced by packing-stones and a pit. They seemed to be placed with unusual regularity, about 6ft between them, and a score were missing. The circle was carefully restored and twenty-two stones stand today. They are all broad stones, rather than pillars, and in this the circle is also unusual. Some are triangular topped, some have flat tops, and only two exceed 3ft above ground. A cairn is sited 100yd away to the east.

The only example on Dartmoor of two circles close together are those known as the Grey Wethers, near Sittaford Tor, on the ridge dividing the North and South Teign rivers. They are 20ft apart at their nearest point and are carefully sited, on an almost level shelf of ground, downhill eastwards from the tor. At 1,550ft above sea level they are as high as White Moor circle, and with diameters of 116ft (south) and 103ft (north) they are the largest and third largest circles on the Moor respectively. Fine views south to Bellever Tor, and beyond to the high ridges of southern Dartmoor, emphasise the dramatic setting.

The pair of circles may be compared with the inner circles at Avebury, where the southern circle is also the larger, and both are made of unworked blocks of stone. Unlike Avebury, however, there is no great circle or bank enclosing the area of the circles, no stone avenue of approach, and no trace of a shrine inside a circle has been found at Grey Wethers or at any other Dartmoor circle.

The northern circle is considerably restored, but the southern has retained most of its original stones. In both circles they are unusually similar in size and shape. The majority of them are so rectangular that they appear to have been worked; but Worth pointed out that similar blocks can be found scattered in the area, and there can be no doubt of their natural origin.

The circles were examined by the Exploration Committee, and wood charcoal was found strewn on the sub-soil floor. This discovery followed the finding of quantities of charcoal at the Fernworthy circle and was evidence of considerable fires, whether for funeral or other rites, or for actual cremations, is not known. Belief that the circles had a sepulchral purpose led the explorers to make a careful search for cairns in the area of the Grey Wethers. Two mounds rising only a few inches above the surface, which might otherwise have been missed, proved to be unviolated cairns covering pits with charcoal. Fires, and a few cairns over cremations not far away, are unfortunately the only indication of the use of the Dartmoor circles.

The most impressive circle on the Moor today is undoubtedly that at Scorhill (page 125), a few hundred yards north of the meeting of the North Teign and its tributary Wallabrook. Samuel Rowe (1848) considered it 'by far the finest example of the rude but venerable shrines of Druidical worship in Devonshire'. The site is at 1,200ft near the bottom of a gentle south-west slope where the ground levels out towards the Wallabrook. It is more in a valley than any other circle, but the valley being the great basin drained by the North Teign and its tributaries, the circle can be seen from considerable

142

Page 143 (above) Bronze rapier from Fice's Well; flint axe of Neolithic type from Cosdon Hill, stone axe-hammer from near Crockern Tor, and bronze spear ferrule from Gawler Bottom; *(below)* flints: Bronze Age arrowhead from northern Dartmoor and Wessex arrowheads found at Grimspound and Chittaford Down; scrapers from kists at Lakehead Hill and Merrivale; early Bronze Age arrowhead; long leaf-shaped arrowheads (Neolithic) from northern Dartmoor

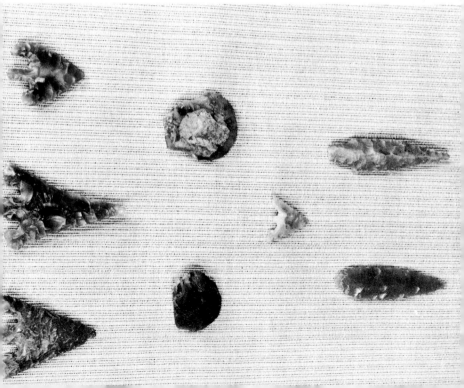

Page 144 The large hut in the Round Pound at Kestor was found by excavation to have been an Iron Age smithy

distances. A vast horseshoe of hills and tors—Buttern, Kennon and Cosdon Hills in the north, Watern and Wild Tors to the west, and Kestor in the south-east—look down on the site. Its unique features are that it has not been restored, and the stones are laid out in a more perfect circle than usual.

The remains have not altered since Worth surveyed them in 1931. The diameter is 88ft, marked by twenty-three erect stones and seven fallen. The largest stands over 8ft above ground, the largest stone to survive in any circle on Dartmoor. Another seven are over 4ft high and only five are less than 3ft. Pillars and triangular slabs are noticeable among them. Probably two dozen stones have been taken away.

Some of the missing stones were used to form the lower bank of the leat which runs close to the circle. They can still be seen and vary in length from nearly 5ft to over 8ft. With these and other fallen or missing stones, the original circle must have been an impressive monument.

The fate that might have overtaken Scorhill is well illustrated by the vestiges of a circle of slightly smaller diameter (81ft) sited only 1,300yd to the north-west. At the foot of Buttern Hill, on the south side of the saddle between it and Kennon Hill, is a scene of almost total destruction. Only five small stones remain in position, three upright and two leaning. Strewn about the denuded surface, in positions where most of them could not have fallen naturally, lie another fourteen stones. There are also four or five very small pieces of granite which were probably triggers for stones that have vanished. About thirty are missing. Some of those that have survived are not in their original condition, having been worked on by masons. The site is not dissimilar to Scorhill, though the view is more limited. The survival of Scorhill in its present form appears miraculous when contemplating the sad ruin at Buttern Hill.

STANDING STONES

Large undressed stones standing by themselves are rare on Dartmoor. Considering the suitable blocks strewn widely over the Moor, and contrasted with the many fine examples known not far away in Cornwall, this is surprising. Some have no doubt disappeared—taken for gate posts or bridges or other mundane purposes—and some may lie fallen and unrecognised.

They do not seem to have attracted the earlier explorers, and the first account was a paper by Worth as recently as 1940. Burials have been found near the base of these stones, elsewhere, but nothing has so far been recorded on Dartmoor. If not associated with burials, they must have been objects of devotion round which ceremonies of some sort took place. Excavation has shown that they were usually manoeuvred into prepared pits and wedged upright by small stones.

The stone on White Moor, within 200yd of the restored circle, is a typical Dartmoor enigma. It stands 5½ft above ground and marks the meeting of South Tawton–Throwleigh parish boundary with Lydford, ie the Forest of Dartmoor. Worth questioned whether it had been erected as a boundary mark in historic times; also whether it had been taken from the stone circle for this purpose.

The explorers of the circle found only one gap in it, and the missing stone had been dressed before removal, the chippings lying near the hole. White Moor stone is of undressed granite so there is no place in the circle from which it could have been taken. This appears to support its prehistoric origin as a standing stone associated with a circle.

But its erection as a boundary mark in historic times is also a possibility. The original Forest boundary ran from Cosdon Hill to Little Hound Tor (Hound Tor on OS maps), and the White Moor stone is to the east of this line. It is not mentioned in any of the perambulations and surveys of the Forest bounds down to the seventeenth century. At some time during the last three hundred years the boundary has been altered, South Tawton Common encroaching on the Forest. The line now runs south-east from the junction of Smallbrook and Taw to White Moor stone, and then turns south-west to Little Hound Tor. The stone is an important turning point in the new boundary and could have been erected for this purpose. Its prehistoric origin is therefore at least suspect.

The stone on Lee Moor (584637) was also once used as a boundary mark of some kind, the letters CB being incised one on top of the other on its eastern face. Their significance is not known. But Worth considered the stone a genuine 'menhir' and so it seems. It leans out of vertical by nearly 40° and has long been called the Hanging or Leaning Rock. If erect it would stand nearly 8ft above ground, a substantial pillar twice as broad as thick at its base and tapering only a little towards the top. No other remains are associated with it, but the surrounding area contains many relics of prehistoric man.

By contrast, the slightly leaning stone near Harbourne Head is a fine triangular slab. It stands over 8ft above ground, tapering to a short flat top, and is barely a foot thick overall. The proportion between breadth and thickness has a rough similarity to human dimensions. The triangular shape may— as in stone rows—indicate a female rather than a male symbol. It has all the appearance of a prehistoric stone in spite of a bench mark incised on one side.

The most impressive of the recorded standing stones is the tall pillar known as Beardown Man (page 125). Situated far up the Cowsic, close to the insignificant rocks of Devil's Tor, its remoteness and the wild beauty of the surroundings enhance its mystery. Nearly 11½ft above ground, it is more than 3ft higher than any of the others. Like the stone near Har-

147

bourne Head, it is markedly thin in proportion to its breadth, appearing as a substantial pillar from in front or behind, but more like a needle from the side. In contrast to the triangular slab, the male symbolism is clear. There is little doubt that this was an important object to prehistoric man.

Among the recumbent stones scattered over the Moor there are two (659593), half a mile north-east of the summit of Butterdon Hill, which seem likely to have been, or were intended to be, genuine standing stones. They lie some 60yd apart on grass moorland where only a few small surface stones are visible. They must have been brought to this spot, probably from the area of Hangershell Rock, the nearest clatter. Both measure 18ft or over and are therefore longer than any tall stone on Dartmoor. The tallest known is a terminal to one of the stone rows at Drizzlecombe (page 126) and was 17ft 10in when fallen and 14ft above ground when re-erected. If the great pillars on Butterdon were erected they would stand over 14ft above ground and would compare favourably with the best surviving examples elsewhere.

8

SANCTUARIES

Groups of monuments at a few places on the Moor, though not to be compared in grandeur with the great Bronze Age sanctuaries of Wessex, can only properly be so described. Shovel Down, Fernworthy, Merrivale and Drizzlecombe (Figs 14A & 14B) have been mentioned in previous chapters because no account of Bronze Age remains on Dartmoor is possible without reference to them. Kist burials are associated with all four, and such finds as have been made are all of Beaker relics. Though there is little direct evidence, the sanctity of such special sites is likely to have been observed over a long period.

Shovel Down is a complex group of rows and cairns laid out on both slopes of the low ridge which runs south-west from Kestor. The rows on the northern slope are therefore not intervisible with those on the southern. But there seems no doubt that they constituted one coherent group, the higher terminals on each side being only a short distance apart near the top of the ridge.

The centre of the northern group is now a cairn with four circles of stones, the outermost having a diameter of 30ft. A double row leads to it from the north. It runs for nearly 200yd up a gentle slope but the lower section has almost disappeared —no doubt used to form Batworthy enclosure wall. Some

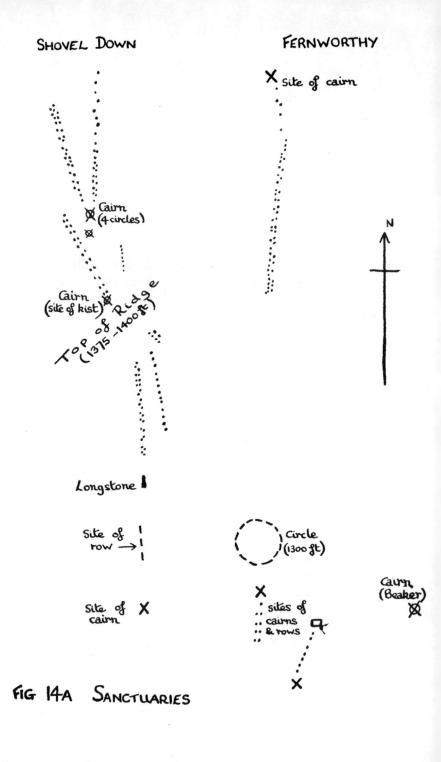

SHOVEL DOWN

FERNWORTHY

X site of cairn

Cairn
(4 circles)

Cairn
(site of kist)

Top of Ridge
(1375-1400ft)

Longstone

Site of row →

Circle
(1300 ft)

Cairn
(Beaker)

Site of cairn X

sites of cairns & rows

N

FIG 14A SANCTUARIES

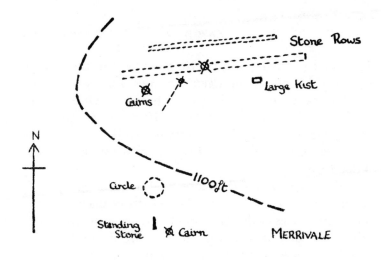

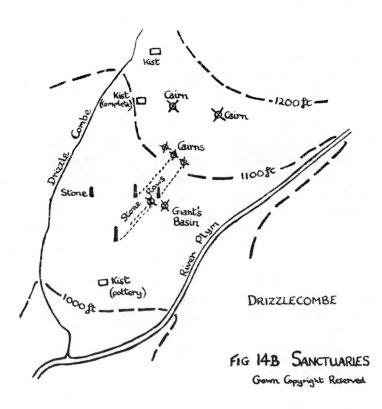

FIG 14B SANCTUARIES

forty stones remain, and twelve pairs next to the cairn indicate a width of $3\frac{1}{2}$ft between the lines. Immediately adjoining the cairn are two large fallen stones. One is a pillar $11\frac{1}{2}$ft long, the other a slab over 7ft with one end broadly triangular in shape. These stones probably stood facing each other, forming a fine pair of the contrasting shapes noted in other rows.

This first row was therefore typical, running up a slight slope to a cairn and with the largest stones placed next to it. The four circles of the cairn, however, are unusual. The only other example, at Yellowmead, has already been described and is a more grandiose conception altogether.

Some 20yds north-west of the cairn a second double row begins and can be traced north-west for 160yd. Neither end is defined by cairn or tall stone, though a small and devastated cairn, 20yds south of the principal cairn, is almost in line with the row and may have been its southern terminal. Some forty stones survive, including nine pairs. The direction of the row converges southwards on the first row.

A third row begins about 15yds west of the principal cairn and climbs the slope south-eastwards to a cairn below the top of the ridge. A kist was formerly recorded in this cairn. With a length of 130yd, and seventy stones remaining, including many pairs, this is the best preserved of the northern rows. It is also typical, straggling up the slope with a varying width between the lines, and the direction converging southwards on both the other rows.

East of this third row, at a distance of about 40yd narrowing to 25yd, a single row of twenty small stones can be traced. Neither end of the row is defined. However, it does conform with the pattern of the three double rows, ie it converges on them in the direction of the ridge.

Missing cairns and stones suggest that some features of the

northern group may have disappeared altogether, or be no longer recognisable. For example, three broad stones not far from the second row are apparently set on the same circumference and could be the remains of a cairn or small stone circle. Excavation here might still be worth while.

The rows on the southern slopes of Shovel Down are even more devastated than the northern ones, and the original pattern is difficult to trace. The best preserved row is double and leads up to the top of the ridge. The higher end is not now marked, but it probably led to a cairn situated not far from the recorded kist in the northern group. This row can be traced southwards for about 160yd. Fifty stones survive, the pairs set rather closer, and the stones generally smaller, than in the best rows of the northern group. The lower end is marked by the well-known Longstone, a tall stone standing over ten feet above ground (page 126).

A short distance east of the double row, and converging on it towards the north, the remains of a single row without defined ends are visible. Northwards of it a few stones, apparently part of a double row, are set in a line which converges on it and on the double row. Thus three rows of the southern group appear to have formed a roughly similar pattern to the northern group, ie all converging towards the top of the ridge.

South from the Longstone another double row formerly existed. This arrangement, of one tall stone marking the end of two rows, is unusual. In 1858 it was recorded that the pits from which the stones of this southern row had been removed were still visible, and they have been traced again recently. The row was about 220yd long and terminated at three substantial stones known as The Three Boys. They were once thought to be the remains of a burial chamber, but were probably tall stones next to a vanished cairn, or part of a cairn circle, at the lower end of the row. Only one 'Boy' remains today, leaning close to the ground. When vertical it would have stood to a height of five to six feet above ground.

If Shovel Down today is a mere remnant, some idea of its past grandeur can still be gleaned from the fine Longstone, the four-fold cairn circle with the fallen tall stones next to it, and, imaginatively, by the sweep of the converging rows. Eight important tombs at least must have existed here.

By contrast, the sanctuary at Fernworthy is on almost level ground. The centre is a well preserved stone circle from which all the rest of the group would have been visible. Although the stones in the circle are small—the largest is only 3½ft high—twenty-seven stones are standing and clearly defined out of an original twenty-nine or thirty. The diameter is 64ft and the circumference almost a true circle.

The group was explored in 1897. Under 18in of peat in the circle, the sub-soil floor was found to be strewn with pieces of charcoal. It was recorded that 'every scoop of pick and shovel' produced charcoal. This evidence of considerable fires was also found later at the Grey Wethers.

The group is unusual in having rows associated with the circle. About 100yd north of the circle the remains of a double row begin and run north towards the site of a cairn. Over forty small stones remain, more than half of them in pairs, and covering a distance of 60yd. The southern end of the row is not defined and it probably extended nearer to the circle.

South and south-east of the circle were two short double rows, now vanished, except for a few stones in the western-most which led to a cairn close to the circumference of the circle. The other short row, with cairns at both ends, has disappeared in the modern plantation. One of these cairns

154

rewarded the explorers. It was already wasted and pillaged, only two sides of a kist remaining, but in the kist a lot of burnt bone was mixed with peaty earth and sub-soil, also some charcoal. This, and the burnt bone found in the small kist on Langstone Moor, are the best evidence for the adoption of cremation by the Beaker people. It is interesting that the two discoveries were made on opposite sides of the Moor. The other cairns at Fernworthy had pits in the sub-soil, not kists, indicating changing customs and long use of the sanctuary. As at Shovel Down, the rows all had a different axis, though aligned north-east towards cairns within an arc of 20°.

Further evidence of a change of custom was found not far away. A cairn standing by itself, east-south-east of the circle, the remains of which can still be seen, proved to be undisturbed and yielded important finds. The sub-soil had been excavated to a depth of 14in to form a floor, and then a pit dug 18in deep and covered by two flat stones. The stones of the cairn had been heaped over this. In time the covers caved in and the pit became full of stones. On one of the coverstones lay a piece of bronze, $1\frac{1}{2}$in long, with fragments of wood adhering to it. This was the remains of a dagger and its wooden handle. Under the cover stones, and crushed by their subsidence, was a beaker.

When restored (see plate, page 90) the beaker stood $7\frac{1}{2}$in high and had a diameter of 3in at the base and 5in at the rim. The tall neck and rounded body are characteristic of the type known as Necked Beakers. They are known from many sites in Britain, but have no counterpart on the Continent.

The decoration of the beaker is by incised lines, vertical, horizontal, and oblique, including hatching, and there is a striking and characteristic pattern of chevrons at the base. The decoration covers nearly all the surface of the vessel.

155

This is the only beaker (or beaker–fragments) found on Dartmoor other than in a kist.

Among the pottery fragments was a flint knife which had probably been placed in the beaker, also a dress-fastener or button of lignite with a V perforation for its cord. These items and the piece of bronze and wood fragments make up the best collection of objects to be recovered from a grave on Dartmoor. Charcoal also was found in the pit, but no trace of bone or burnt bone. The acid soil, and furze roots reaching to the bottom of the pit, had no doubt destroyed any evidence of the actual interment.

Merrivale also has a circle associated with rows and is sited on comparatively level ground. A glance at a contoured map shows how carefully the site was chosen. The remains occupy the best piece of level ground anywhere close to the Walkham. Below them the hill falls steeply to the river. Here survive three stone rows, five cairns, a circle and a standing stone, all intervisible today as they were 3500 years ago.

The group has attracted attention ever since a first attempt was made to describe it in 1802. Many conflicting and inadequate reports followed, each suggesting some former cairn or row which cannot now be seen. In 1895 the Exploration Committee examined the site. The coverstone of the large kist, which had hitherto been regarded as a chambered tomb, was raised and the true nature of the burial disclosed. The finds inside were recorded simply as 'a flint scraper, a flint flake, and a polishing stone'. The latter is a whetstone for sharpening metal implements.

Close to the stone circle several pits twelve to eighteen inches deep were found, a flint flake in one of them. They were thought to be sockets for more stones, but they could well have been pits for burials, or for ritual deposits similar to those associated with sanctuaries in Wessex. Only one sad fact emerges from these accounts: the surviving stones are but vestiges of a great Beaker monument, the complete plan of which is probably lost for ever.

The two main rows run east and west some thirty yards apart and, diverging by only $2\frac{1}{2}°$, look parallel. There is no other example on Dartmoor of rows forming an avenue like this. A leat, constructed between them during the nineteenth century, is no longer maintained and the water artificially brought to the site overflows and creates a morass. These wet conditions should be ignored when considering the monument.

The northern row is 180yd in length, a double row with some 160 stones remaining, many of them very small. Fifty-five pairs indicate that the space between the lines varied in the usual way. The course of the row is irregular. The slightly higher end is marked by a substantial transverse slab, but at the lower end there is nothing, no stone or cairn or trace of a cairn.

The southern row is 100yd longer, projecting beyond the northern row at both ends. Over 200 stones can be counted though many are very small. Seventy-five pairs show, as in the other row, a varying though smaller space between the lines. It also has a transverse stone at the higher end, a fine triangular slab, and nothing at the lower end. However, two largish stones of familiar shapes, a pillar and a broad slab, form the last pair at the lower end and may indicate the former presence of a cairn. The unique feature of this row is a cairn of 12ft diameter, marked by a circle of stones and with traces of a kist, roughly midway along it. No other row on Dartmoor is interrupted in this way.

The third row at Merrivale is single and short—a mere seven stones and a terminal stone marking a distance of 40yd. It leads to a very small cairn sited a few yards from the southern double row. The alignment diverges more than 50° from that of the double row. Perhaps this exceptional divergence was due to the level site, choice of direction not being governed by gradient, though similar conditions at Fernworthy were apparently not used in this way.

Within a short distance of the southern double row is another ruined cairn and also the large kist already mentioned. A little further south lies the stone circle. With a diameter of 62ft it is one of the smaller ones, similar to that at Fernworthy. The eleven remaining stones are small, as at Fernworthy. They appear to be short pillars alternating with broad stones with flat tops.

Close to the circle is a fine standing stone, 10½ft above ground. South-east of this lies a ruined cairn, and beyond this, and in the same line, a smaller single stone. This was re-erected in 1895 and has since fallen again. It is doubtful whether it was ever a true monolith: more likely a substantial stone in a row or cairn circle. A few set stones scattered about the ground here and close to the standing stone may be the relics of rows or cairn circles. Much has obviously been destroyed. But with the abandoned leat running through the double rows, and the main road only a few hundred yards away, perhaps it is remarkable that so much of Merrivale remains.

Worth rated the group of cairns and rows at Drizzlecombe (sqs 5966/5967) the most important on Dartmoor, and no one will disagree with him. In spite of obvious possible extensions, it has a simplicity and air of cohesion not achieved or surviving elsewhere. Add to this its lonely setting, three miles up the Plym from Cadover Bridge, and there is no doubt that this is the most impressive prehistoric site on the Moor.

A cairn 58ft in diameter forms the north-east and highest point of the group. Below it the remains extend down the gentle south-west slope between the Plym and the stream which gives the combe its name.

Near the cairn are four enclosed settlements, intrusive on the monument. The wall of one passes only a few yards from the cairn and is imposed between it and three other cairns which lie 170yd south-west. These cairns are close together in a line and form the base of a long triangle with roughly equal sides of which the principal cairn marks the top. Leading up to the central and southernmost of the three cairns are stone rows which converge sufficiently to point at the principal cairn, as well as at the cairn to which they lead. Perhaps a row to the northernmost cairn was planned, similarly aligned on the principal cairn. A substantial stone, all by itself, 330yd south-west of the northernmost cairn, is in the right position to mark the beginning of such a row.

The rows are single, and each has at the lower end an imposing terminal stone. One stands 14ft above ground and is the tallest erect stone on Dartmoor (page 126). Both rows, therefore, have an orthodox plan: a cairn at the higher end, a large stone at the lower, but the latter are exceptionally large.

A third row lies below and roughly in the same line as the row leading to the southernmost of the three cairns. This row also has a fine stone, 10½ft above ground at the lower end, and leads up to a cairn. Part of it is single and part double, which appears to be the way it was built. The higher section is double, as in the similar row at Glasscombe Ball.

Nowhere else can three rows be seen with such massive terminal stones. Close to the rows is a large cairn, a great heap of stones with a diameter of 70ft, known as Giant's Basin. The centre has been hollowed out, hence its name, and the circumference may have been enlarged by stones thrown down from the top. Nothing is known about its purpose or whether

159

it had any connection with the sanctuary or was a later intrusion. But there are records and remains of other cairns near to the rows which were clearly Beaker burials. A pillaged kist 150yd south of the lowest row had only two sides remaining when explored in 1900. Two fragments of plain pottery were found in it, all that remained of a beaker of unknown type. (This kist, Giant's Basin, and the focal cairn of the group are in a straight line. Another cairn is sited in line with one of the three cairns and with Giant's Basin. Such geometrical patterns can only have significance if Giant's Basin was contemporary.)

Two other kists, north of the sanctuary, were well preserved—one complete and the other with only its coverstone missing, as can be seen today. Except for a few fragments of charcoal in the latter, digging yielded no results. Yet another cairn, close to the complete kist, had a continuous circle of flat stones round half the circumference, and yielded a well-made disc-shaped scraper of Beaker type.

Both record and result of investigations at Drizzlecombe were meagre. But the early explorers deserve the visitor's gratitude for re-erecting the tall stones. All three were put back in their socket holes in 1893, though it was found necessary to deepen the original holes. It is these great undressed pillars of granite which make Drizzlecombe an impressive monument still.

9
BRONZE AGE FINDS —
CONCLUSION

A few objects have been found on Dartmoor not associated with settlements or burials. They represent the whole span of the Bronze Age.

In 1905 a stone axe-hammer was discovered near Crockern Tor by a labourer taking stone for the main road. The Prince of Wales, says the report, rewarded the finder 'very liberally'. The tool lay 18in below the surface, under a granite slab, and only a few yards from the road. It is a good specimen, 5½in long, with a shaft hole tapering towards the middle, ie it had been drilled from both sides (page 143). Such axes have been found in other places associated with beakers. This example is therefore additional evidence of the presence of the Beaker people in the West Dart valley.

A knife of pale grey flint, 4½in long, was found near Cullever Steps (East Okement) in 1935. It was picked up on the surface after heavy rain. This, too, was probably Beaker. The top half of a similar though larger blade had been found a few years previously in the Avon valley. These finds were in areas where Beaker remains are scarce, and suggest that the Beaker people roamed widely over the Moor.

Some fine flint arrowheads were collected before World War I on Northern Dartmoor by an Okehampton solicitor,

J. D. Prickman (page 143). Unfortunately there is no record of where and when they were found. They are barbed and tanged, some with curved sides, others straight-sided and tri-angular in shape. Some of these may be Beaker or main Bronze Age weapons, but the finely worked triangular ones are of Wessex type, ie attributable to the culture which succeeded the Beaker culture in Wessex and which is represented on Dartmoor by the cairns on Hameldown.

Other Wessex type arrowheads have been found at Fern-worthy (exact locality not known), Postbridge (Chittaford Down) and Grimspound (page 143). All have barbs equal in length to the tang and are finely worked. The one from Grimspound was picked up on the surface after heavy rain, like the knife at Cullever Steps. It can probably be attributed to the builders of the Hameldown cairns, ante-dating the enclosed settlement by several hundred years.

Spindle-whorls have been found away from surviving settle-ments. One made of slate was picked up at Leedon Tor to-wards the end of the last century. It probably came from one of the settlements nearby. Some good examples made of both slate and sandstone have been recorded recently at Welstor on the south-east edge of the Moor. Others have been found near Widecombe.

An outstanding find of bronze, probably only equalled in interest by the palstave from Horridge Common, was made in 1906 by an inmate of Dartmoor prison. A new road was being made on the prison farm near Fice's Well, north of the Two Bridges–Tavistock road. One of the working party turned up a well preserved bronze rapier (page 143). It was 18in long and had rivet holes for attaching it to its missing hilt. It was found buried under 18in of apparently undisturbed peat and lay flat on the black soil beneath. Embedded in the soil were roots and boles of oak trees. The area must once have been covered by oak forest or scrub, and the rapier dropped after clearance but before the peat began to form. It was not associated with any known settlement or grave and is unlikely to have been buried deliberately.

Several similar rapiers are recorded from other parts of Devon. Stone moulds for making them were discovered in 1852 in the Teign valley, a few miles off the Moor. They are characteristic weapons of main Bronze Age times, evolved from the fine daggers of the Wessex culture as found at Hameldown. They were eventually replaced by heavier, broader swords introduced from the Continent but not represented on Dartmoor. The rapier at Fice's Well therefore seems to have been dropped some time between 1200–900 BC.

Somewhat similar was the dagger or small dirk found under 2ft of peat near Broadhall Head (Yealm). It was slightly over 4in long, slender and sharp pointed. It looked exactly like a small rapier, though first recorded as a lance-head. This too was well preserved and may have been of similar date to the rapier from Fice's Well; but the making of such weapons could have gone on for a long period.

Of later Bronze Age times is the ferrule of a bronze spearhead from Gawler Bottom (sq 6377—page 143), the boggy area north of the Postbridge–Two Bridges road between Archerton and Cherrybrook. It was found in 1892 when peat was being cut, and lay 4ft below the surface. Roots of trees and bushes were found, as at Fice's Well, indicating that the valley had been covered in scrub or forest before the peat began to form. Normally, ferrules were fastened to the shaft by a pin but this one was broken off below the pin hole. A similar fragment had been found in 1854 at Bloody Pool, two miles north of South Brent. It was part of a hoard of fine spear-heads, some of which still had pins through the ferrules or showed the pin holes.

163

SUMMARY OF FINDS

Apart from the chance finds described above, the objects from Dartmoor are either grave or domestic goods. It is exasperating that no direct connection between burials and settlements has yet been established. Only in one instance (the cremation on Hurston Ridge) can a find from a cairn be considered as belonging to the same period as the Moor settlements.

The grave goods begin with Beaker burials which, as elsewhere, supply most of our knowledge of these remarkable people. Drinking cups, an archer's wrist guard, finely worked flint knives and arrowheads—these are good evidence of Beaker activity on the Moor. The finds are few compared with the large number of their burials and monuments to survive, and on the whole are unimpressive when compared with finds in other parts of Britain. A kist burial in Yorkshire yielded a bronze dagger, wrist-guard, and a hawk's head arranged round a crouched skeleton. The guard was still in position on the right wrist. A grave in Berkshire contained a beaker, three fine arrowheads, and a pair of gold ear-rings. But the kist at Archerton yielded only a wrist-guard, thrust to one side by pillagers, and a single flint. The difficulty on Dartmoor has been to find undisturbed burials. The knives and scrapers from the kist on Lakehead Hill had fortunately been ignored when treasure-seekers wrecked the tomb and shattered a beaker into thirty fragments. Three arrowheads and a broken beaker from one of the kists at Deadman's Bottom had also been of no importance to the pillagers. However, when Burnard found an intact beaker in the unpillaged kist on Chagford Common, it was not accompanied by any other object. The finds in the undisturbed cairn at Fernworthy—bronze dagger, beaker, flint knife, lignite button—were therefore exceptional for Dartmoor. The tiny piece of corroded bronze in the plundered kist at Raddick Hill was typical of the disappointments endured by the early explorers. Without robbery, and without the corrosive action of the soil, some more objects might have been found.

The Beaker people introduced inhumation in circular cairns, the interment in the centre. But at two places (Fernworthy, Langstone Moor) the presence of burnt bone in kists indicates that sooner or later they adopted the practice of cremation. The beaker from a pit with charcoal at Fernworthy is further evidence of this. As Beaker dominance declined, it seems that cremation became general. The idea of placing the dead in a circle persisted, but interment was not always central in the cairn.

The distinctive cremations on Hameldown may have taken place while kist burial was still going on elsewhere on the Moor (c 1550 BC). Similar burials are known at other places in Devon, but these cairns are the only evidence at present of the Wessex culture reaching Dartmoor. Arrowheads of Wessex type, found at Fernworthy and elsewhere, seem to denote trade with Beaker–Neolithic inhabitants rather than occupation. The Hameldown dagger with its gold-pinned amber pommel was the richest find ever to be made on Dartmoor. What a pity that it is now only known from photographs.

With the Bronze Age fully established (from 1400 BC) the evidence from graves is much less positive. It is known from many sites in Britain that cremations were often inserted in existing cairns (secondary burial), but there is no record of this on Dartmoor—unless the layout of one of the cairns on Soussons Common can be so interpreted. It is also known that grave goods became of less importance and that only meagre objects were deposited with the ashes. Cairns covering pits may be attributed to this period. Certainly the finds in them, pillaged or unpillaged, have been negligible: flint flakes or fragments (Stannon Bottom, Hemstone Rocks), fragment of bronze (Soussons Common), a piece of slate for modelling clay (Pen Beacon). The two undisturbed cairns, near the Grey Wethers, yielded no objects at all.

Only one burial can be dated by pottery to this period—the cremation on Hurston Ridge. This type of interment, with a large urn inverted over ashes, was widespread in Britain during main Bronze Age times. It is therefore remarkable that only one example has been recorded on Dartmoor, where so many settlements existed in the same period. Perhaps some urns have been destroyed by natural causes, or their decayed fragments scattered or crushed by pillagers.

In any event, burial ritual was declining. Carefully constructed pits like the ones at Hemstone Rocks and Stannon Bottom are outnumbered by simple holes in the sub-soil (Holne Moor) and mere scooped depressions (Hemstone Rocks, White Hill). Eventually, the old rituals seem to have been given up altogether: no more cairns were built over the ashes of dead leaders, no objects interred with the remains. It is difficult to assess when this happened. No doubt it was a gradual process, perhaps already in progress in main Bronze Age times, and apparently general after 900 BC.

The finds in settlements have also been few compared with the number of sites examined. Other than pottery, they are a mixture of the ordinary and unusual. Most explorations revealed water-worn stones used for cooking, though some of these (eg pebbles at Standon) may have been for parching grain before storing, to prevent germination. Flints, and charcoal from hearths, were universal. None of these finds indicate a specific date, merely a primitive society compatible with Bronze Age times. Ordinary but more significant finds came from a few settlements, eg charred wood from pottery-baking pits at Har Tor village, and querns and grain rubbers at

166

Dean Moor, Yes Tor Bottom, and possibly Standon village, which indicated cultivation. Spindle-whorls—clay at Legis Tor, shale at Dean Moor—suggest that spinning and weaving were general. Whetstones for sharpening metal tools, and therefore not to be dated before the Bronze Age, were found at Riders Rings, Legis Tor, Har Tor village and Dean Moor. Attempts to detect particles of bronze on the sharpening surfaces of specimens from Dean Moor were not successful.

Not even a fragment of bronze has been found in a hut. The remarkable palstave from Horridge Common is the only bronze object so far associated with settlement. The lack of bronze led early explorers to think that the settlements must have pre-dated the use of metal. Even the modern techniques used at Kestor and Dean Moor did not uncover any bronze.

The significance of tin ore and slag at Dean Moor has already been emphasised, also the lack of ornaments. The rare carnelian beads from Dean Moor provide the only certain glimpse of adornment.

Important finds of pottery came from half a dozen sites. Burnard's cooking pot from Raddick Hill was the only one well enough preserved to permit a complete restoration, but other fragments have sufficed to disclose the shape and ornamentation of the original vessels. Pottery is at present the only guide to occupation dates on the Moor. This is not a satisfactory method because particular types of vessels were used over long periods, and for different periods in different areas. Dates deduced solely from pottery cannot therefore be absolute.

Recent excavations at two sites in Cornwall (Trevisker and Gwithian) have given the best basis so far for dating Bronze Age pottery in the South West. Briefly, the Cornish sequence shows that ornamentation by plaited-cord impressions was used on the earliest pottery; and this was followed by predominantly twisted-cord impressions combined with incised

167

decoration, ribs to strengthen bases, and flat cordons. Cord ornamentation subsequently died out, and incised decoration, often broad and rough, continued. These styles covered the whole period of the main Bronze Age 1400–900 BC; but it is apparent that they could still have been in use in some places during later centuries.

The only records on Dartmoor of plaited-cord impressions are from Watern Oke and Dean Moor. In both cases they are decayed fragments, the one from Dean Moor with a single line made by a plait of three thongs. They can probably be dated from c 1400 BC. Fragments indicating a later date, from other huts at Dean Moor, ie with twisted-cord impressions and incised grooves, suggest a long period of occupation. Unfortunately no stratified layers have been established on Dartmoor, and continuous occupation of a site or single hut for several centuries should preferably be based on these. Nevertheless, the pastoral economy of the settlements was clearly maintained over long periods; and at Dean Moor the carnelian beads suggest that the inhabitants had another aid to survival, ie tin, to offer to traders who came to the south coast from the Continent and the Mediterranean.

Twisted-cord ornament has been found on fragments from several settlements. The most impressive examples came from the farm at Smallacombe Rocks, with festoon and interlocking zigzag patterns in addition to the more common horizontal and oblique lines. The unusual zigzag design was also noted on the fragments, now lost, from Broadmoor Pound. At Yes Tor Bottom pieces with cord ornament were associated with a reinforced base, another type feature. The record of a single sherd with cord ornament, from Standon village, confirms that this type of settlement was contemporary with enclosed settlements and the earliest farms.

The small vessel found recently near the Dewerstone settlement is unlike any other from Dartmoor and does not fit into the Cornish sequence. Indeed, nothing exactly similar is known anywhere, though it is related to urns from Dorset and Cornwall, and 'dimple' decoration has been found in Somerset. A date c 1300 BC is suggested for it, ie when cord ornament predominated.

Pottery with incised decoration comes from seven settlements, including Dean Moor. Burnard's vessel from Raddick Hill, with crude chevrons between the rim and a heavy cordon, is typical of this group and may be dated between 1300–1000 BC. Similar incised chevrons above cordons were found at Legis Tor, Tunhill Rocks and Har Tor village. A rather different chevron pattern, with the strokes not meeting, comes from Foales Arrishes farm. Again it is clear that the three main types of settlement shared a common culture. Stabbed or broken-line chevrons, incised with a comb, are rarer. They are recorded only from Legis Tor and one of the White Ridge farms.

CONCLUSION

With such few and fragmentary finds, the problem of accurate dating of the settlements is far from being solved. Such evidence as exists indicates that the majority of the settlements flourished in the main period of the Bronze Age (1400–900 BC). Some may have earlier origins—for example, small enclosed settlements, with three huts or less, could represent a first stage of colonisation—and some undoubtedly continued in use through the first half of the first millenium BC.

Why and when were the majority of settlements abandoned? It is known that the climate deteriorated dramatically after 900 BC, and that peat growth increased in very wet conditions. No pottery from settlements can at present be dated confidently after this date and before the early Iron Age. Of course, upland communities could maintain themselves without interference, and without change in pottery styles, over long periods, even if conditions reduced them in size and number. But the lack of later Bronze Age pottery, and the change of climate, do suggest that the majority of settlements ceased to be used before the end of Bronze Age times. Another factor may have been the exhaustion of surface tin, the only supply accessible to prehistoric man.

The finds in settlements do not include any really important object of domestic use, only trifles which could have been left because they were not worth taking away (flint scraps and pots in holes), or have been dropped accidentally (the beads at Dean Moor). No evidence has been forthcoming of conquest—no deliberate destruction of huts or litter of weapons. Only two or three huts have yielded an arrowhead. Even allowing for destruction by time and soil of many objects, the impression is that settlements were peacefully abandoned, the inhabitants departing with their goods and chattels. This would explain the lack of bronze objects—they were too valuable to be discarded; only scraps would be left to be destroyed by time and soil. Some settlements were no doubt stricken by natural disasters, and some would certainly have been deserted earlier on while new ones were still being established. Abandonment must have been a long drawn out process, against a background of deteriorating conditions. In this way, it seems, the important period of the Moor's prehistory came to an end.

10

IRON AGE

Archaeologists are undecided how far the introduction of iron-working to Britain was due to immigration from the Continent, and how far to infiltration of knowledge along the Bronze Age trade routes. Probably some immigrants using iron tools, and with experience of iron-working, did arrive about the middle of the first millenium BC and continued to arrive in small numbers during the next two or three centuries (Iron Age A). Being agriculturists, they were easily absorbed by the native population. But the knowledge which they brought was revolutionary and was to dominate the making of tools and weapons until modern times.

These immigrants, and later more numerous intruders (Iron Age B), were the first to be given a generic name—the Celts. By contact with Mediterranean civilisations such as the Etruscan and Roman, they entered recorded history; but in Britain, until the coming of the Romans, they formed the last prehistoric society.

At Dean Moor the discovery of iron ore indicated that Bronze Age people recognised the mineral but were unable to work it. Possibly this was because a higher temperature was necessary to smelt iron than to smelt tin. The newcomers used bellows to produce high temperatures, and had discovered the double process by which serviceable iron tools

171

and weapons could be produced. After smelting, the metal had to be forged, ie it was again heated, hammered on an anvil, and then quenched in water. This process was necessary to get rid of impurities and to toughen the metal. It was rather more complicated than bronze working, but the end product was a greatly improved implement, and easy to repair. Moulds were no longer necessary, and the wandering smith of the Bronze Age gave way to blacksmiths who formed an integral part of each community. Bronze was still used, of course, especially for ornamenting weapons and domestic objects.

Iron axes and ploughshares would in time clear many lowland forests, and cultivate areas of heavy soil untouched by hand-digging or wooden ploughs. This would lead to desertion of the highlands generally, but so far as Dartmoor was concerned a fairly general abandonment had apparently already taken place. On the east side, however—always the drier part and with better soil—a few farms at least remained to absorb the new ideas. Some evidence of the arrival of the early Celts here, and of their merging with the existing population, is fortunately available.

At Foales Arrishes farm the Exploration Committee had noted that pottery fragments from one hut were of superior workmanship and material to those from other huts and other settlements. They were found in or about a cooking hole. The largest piece consisted of part of an unthickened rim and side of a vessel down to a thickened shoulder or ridge (carination). Ornament was by finger impressions below the rim, and a row of oblique slashes on the shoulder. The well-baked ware, the shape of rim and shoulder and the ornamentation are now considered to be typical of the earliest Iron Age pottery. Together with pieces of coarser pottery with incised decoration from other huts, the fragments suggest that Foales Arrishes

172

was in use throughout late Bronze Age times, and down to the fourth century BC at least.

The hut in which the Iron Age pottery was found had a diameter of 20ft and an entrance facing south-east. The same size and construction as in hundreds of Bronze Age huts was evident, and this type of dwelling must have been used on Dartmoor over a very long period. It stood in a roughly circular paddock. Huts standing in their own small enclosures, which should be distinguished from enclosed settlements with only one hut, can also be seen at Coombe Down and at Kestor. Excavation of the latter by Lady Fox in 1951–2 yielded remarkable evidence of iron-working on Dartmoor.

The small enclosure has long been known as the Round Pound, though in plan it is a triangle with rounded corners rather than a circle. It stands close to the road to Batworthy, on the hill above the junction of the Batworthy stream with the North Teign river. The site had been roughly levelled into the hillside. The entrance to the enclosure was at the north-west angle of the wall, giving directly on to a droveway that led down between fields to the stream. The entrance way—cobbled, stepped, and flanked by granite slabs laid horizontally—was narrower than that of Grimspound settlement, but otherwise remarkably similar. This appeared to be the only original entrance. Other gaps in the wall were of later date, as also were some walls radiating from the central hut to the enclosure wall. Fragments of medieval pottery found in the hut showed that the Round Pound had been used in historic times.

The hut (page 144) was exceptionally large, 37ft in diameter. (A hut of 39ft on Yar Tor Down is the largest known and is also associated with fields.) The entrance faced south-east and had a cobbled approach. The entrance passage was floored with small stones and flanked by transverse slabs. A step up from the enclosure prevented water from running downhill into the hut. Inside there were three steps down to the floor. Part of the neck of a pottery vessel with fingertip ornamentation was found in the floor at the bottom of the steps.

Large vertical slabs formed the interior wall of the hut, large horizontal slabs the exterior face, and the space between them was filled with small stones. The comparatively well preserved state of the wall was due to its exceptionally solid construction, which had not only withstood the ravages of time and weather but seems also to have discouraged the removal of slabs for other purposes.

The interior of the hut was found to be divided into two distinct sections. On the west side of the entrance the floor was comparatively clean, and there were scattered paving stones embedded in it. A small hearth, with scraps of pottery in the floor beside it, was situated close to the wall. Oak and hazel wood had been burnt. Other finds in this part of the hut were a sandstone spindlewhorl, two hammerstones, several pieces of flint, and pebbles marked by use as rubbers and pounders. A piece of granite 6in broad, standing against the wall, was identified as an anvil. It was worn smooth by use for sharpening, and had a pitted hollow where hammering had taken place. Although the anvil and pebbles were for iron-working, this side of the hut had been the living quarters.

On the other side, dark soil 8–12in deep marked the working quarters and indicated a long period of use. A clay-lined hole in the floor, filled with charcoal and pieces of slag, showed where iron ore had been smelted. This would have been done in a bowl furnace, ie the hole covered over with wet clay. The ore could have come from the Bovey valley about ten miles away. After more than two thousand years, the slag from the last smelting was recovered and carried away to a museum.

Close to the smelting furnace lay a small granite slab. This was thought to be the rest for the bellows used to drive air into the charcoal fire of the furnace.

About 2ft away from the furnace was another small hole filled with ash and charcoal and its base reddened by burning. This was the forging pit where the iron was reheated after smelting. Some 4ft from this, and near the centre of the hut, excavation revealed a shallow depression 3ft in diameter —the drip-pit over which the iron could be quenched with water after being hammered. From the pit a roughly constructed drain ran to the lowest point of the hut wall. It was joined by another short drain from the occupation side of the hut and the combined section was covered by stone slabs.

Careful removal of soil disclosed the positions of a dozen post holes. Another three or four had probably once existed. It did not seem that they formed an inner circle for posts to support a conical roof. Having regard to this, and to the position of the drip-pit near the centre of the hut, it was considered that the roof must have been open somewhere near the centre. This would not only have given light to work by, but would have helped to disperse smoke and fumes. Round this vent the rafters, of varying length and pitch, rested on internal posts. They would have sloped outwards and down—wards and have been firmly bedded in the hut wall. On the working side, one line of posts was sufficient; on the larger occupation side, two lines of holes were identified, the extra support being necessary to carry the larger roof over that section. The roof itself would have been thatched with rushes or heather.

The Round Pound excavation was a landmark in the unveiling of Dartmoor's prehistory. For the first time a large hut standing in its own enclosure was scientifically excavated and evidence discovered of metal-working on the Moor. The only other evidence has been the droplet of tin slag found at Dean Moor a few years later. The results from both these excavations suggest that modern techniques applied to other settlements could still yield important information.

At Kestor a hut on the edge of a field was also examined. It had a diameter of 27ft and was of much better construction than those excavated subsequently at Dean Moor. The paved entrance faced south-west, was only 2ft wide, and had a step down into the hut. The entrance passage was flanked by huge slabs. More than a dozen large slabs, 5ft high and up to 9ft long, formed the inner wall. They were close-set and had drystone walling between the upper parts. The wall was 4–5ft thick, the outer face consisting of smaller slabs and boulders than those on the inside, and the middle filled with small stones as in the Round Pound hut. The site had been levelled by digging into the slope, and on the lower side rather larger boulders were used to form the outer face, and the wall foundations were carefully laid to resist any downhill pressure. As a result, when the hut collapsed, the lower slabs tipped and most of the debris fell uphill. The skill of prehistoric man in selecting and manipulating granite was clearly shown.

Other scattered huts at Kestor seem similarly constructed. Granite on the east side of the Moor has a tendency to split into large slabs, as is apparent at Smallcombe Rocks and Grimspound. This accounts for the massive walls of many farmhouses. Large slabs do not necessarily imply a late date for construction.

The hearth consisted of three stones bedded against the wall opposite the entrance. Both wood and peat had been used for fuel. A scrap of ochre, two quartz crystals, and some disintegrated pottery were found about the hearth. Other

176

finds in the hut were two whetstones and part of a saddle
quern. There were also some more crystals, reminscent of the
find at Broadun enclosed settlement; they may have been
used as pointed implements or as playthings.

A deposit of dark soil above the occupation layer, contemporary with the hut's collapse, may have been the remains of
its turf roof. In the floor, a central hole and an irregular ring
of seven holes between it and the wall were for posts to
support a heavy conical roof. One post hole had pieces of
pottery in it, apparently deliberately broken and placed
there. They belonged to a straight-sided vessel and the texture has been compared with a fragment from a hut at
Foales Arrishes.

The hut stood at the north end of a small yard, the walls of
which joined the hut wall but were not bonded to it. The
west wall curved in towards the hut, so forming a screen for
the entrance. Evidence of cultivation was found in the yard.
To the east was a field, roughly rectangular in shape, and
slightly over half an acre in extent. The longer sides ran down
the slope and were marked by lines of single boulders set
vertically except where the hut and yard walls formed the
boundary. The shorter sides were of thicker construction and
lynchetted by ploughing.

Further evidence of occupation of Dartmoor settlements
during Iron Age A is lacking. Peat had formed over large
areas towards the end of Bronze Age times and the process
continued. Grazing was therefore becoming increasingly
restricted. Nevertheless it seems unlikely that Foales Arrishes
and Kestor were the only farms to survive. Some settlements
on the fringe of the Moor have almost certainly disappeared
altogether in enclosed land, and some of these could have
been occupied in Iron Age times. In the area of Widecombe,
for example, prehistoric objects have been found where

medieval and later occupation would have obliterated other traces of earlier settlement.

At Welstor there is no sign of settlement except for the foundations of an isolated hut; but, among the Mesolithic and Bronze Age objects recently recorded there, was a spindle-whorl of Iron Age pattern. It was incised with a five-pointed star marked out by double curved lines. Comparable whorls have been found at Milber, the Iron Age fort near Newton Abbot, and at Kents Cavern, Torquay. Welstor is only a mile from the extensive field system on Horridge and adjoining Commons, and about the same distance from the Iron Age earthworks at Boro Wood. It seems that a settlement prob-ably existed here for a long period in prehistoric times, though only excavation could establish this, or reveal other settlements on enclosed land.

Forts like Boro Wood were eventually built on many prominent sites all round Dartmoor. Good examples are Cranbrook, Wooston, and Prestonbury above the Teign gorge, and Hembury Castle above the Dart. They are all attributable to a second phase of Celtic immigration (Iron Age B) which began to reach Britain from north-west France in the third century BC. These newcomers, unlike the pre-vious trickle of agricultural settlers, came in large well armed groups. They were warriors seeking land and serfs, and they introduced the horse and the war chariot to Britain. Their characteristic forts, boldly planned on commanding sites, indicate a chronic state of unrest. Some of the mixed Bronze Age and Iron Age A inhabitants, apprehensive at the inroads of these aristocrats, built simple fortifications for protection.

Iron Age ramparts were both earthworks and works of stone construction, or a mixture of both. The sadly-ruined fort at the Dewerstone is an example of stone ramparts. It may have been erected by invading warriors, though there is

178

no evidence (eg finds of pottery of Iron Age B type) of their presence on the Moor. Having regard to the fort's position and simple plan, it seems more likely that it was one of those built as defences against the invaders.

Across the neck of the promontory, where a Bronze Age enclosure already existed, two parallel stone walls were constructed about 9ft apart. At either end the walls curved backwards until the steepness of the slope, perhaps aided by scarping, made them unnecessary. These simply-evolved defences have all the signs of being a place of refuge for people living on Wigford Down, and probably further up the Plym. Evidence there is none, but it is possible that huts in this area were still occupied in Iron Age times. Then, if raiding bands came up the Plym, the natives would have taken refuge with their stock and seeds inside the Dewerstone fort. Attack was only practicable along the promontory, against a short length of wall. A show of defiance would have been sufficient to deter all but large bands under determined leaders.

The only other Iron Age fort on Dartmoor is at White Tor (Tavy). This also has stone ramparts, and is on the western edge, but at 1,500ft it is considerably higher than the Dewerstone fort. Worth described it as a 'prehistoric camp of great interest and of a type unique on Dartmoor'. The Exploration Committee, undaunted by its size and exposed position, tackled it for a week in 1898 and again in March/April 1899 'when weather permitted'.

A double line of ramparts encircles the tor, and in many places, especially on the east side, outcrops of rock are incorporated in them. They are in a ruinous condition, having been built of smallish stones, and enclose an area of one and a half acres. The explorers estimated that the walls were 10–11ft thick, the inner one 6–7ft high and the outer somewhat lower. The space between the walls varied but was

179

generally about 10ft. The entrance appeared to be on the east side where the slope up to the tor is more gradual than on the other sides and where the clatter of boulders which surrounds the tor is least formidable. The gaps in the walls were estimated to be 4ft wide, and the inner one was offset from the outer one and protected by a spur wall.

Inside the fort the foundations of two small buildings were found and some shelters had been built under slabs of rock. The two buildings were close together, one placed on the line of the inner rampart, with a short wall connecting it to the other which lay between the ramparts. This curious arrangement suggests that they were not contemporary with the fort. If previously existing, they would surely have been avoided or destroyed when the ramparts were erected. They must therefore be of later date. The shelters under the rocks are undateable. The fort would only have been a place of refuge in time of danger and would not have been permanently occupied.

The fort also contained some piles of stones similar to cairns. A section of the largest was examined down to ground level, but no indication of its purpose was obtained. Flint chips were found all over the enclosure, suggesting prehistoric use. Fragments of pottery, thought to be both prehistoric and medieval, were also recorded.

Who was responsible for these extraordinary ramparts? The fort is a lofty one, its siting round a tor unique, and the entirely stone construction differs from most of the forts built by the Celts in Devon during the last two centuries BC. White Tor is the centre of an area much used by prehistoric man, witness the many cairns found within half a mile of it, also a stone row, a stone circle, a village, and several enclosed settlements. Is it possible that some Bronze Age pastoralists continued to use the area in Iron Age times and built the fort for refuge against the Celts? Or was it erected by Celts of Iron Age B, perhaps as late as the first century AD, as a tribal stronghold, or even later as a refuge in Roman times? The Celts in Devon submitted to the Romans and survived their occupation, but perhaps some of them sought the western fringe of the Moor for greater independence. Arguments can be used against all these propositions. White Tor is generally accepted as an Iron Age fort, but it keeps its secrets.

As the Iron Age progressed a total lack of knowledge about the Moor has to be admitted. The last Iron Age immigrants (Iron Age C) do not seem to have penetrated to inland Devon west of the Exe. The Moor and its borders must have formed a backwater between the Exe and Tamar. Whether it was entirely abandoned by the last century BC, or whether isolated groups survived into Romano-British times, is not known. The process of abandonment, as towards the end of the Bronze Age, has left no trace. Perhaps some settlements died out; perhaps the inhabitants of others moved off the in-hospitable uplands and accepted slavery under Celtic chiefs. Many hands were necessary to erect the ramparts of the great forts surrounding the Moor. Though none of the Moor settle-ments has yielded evidence of conquest, raids by horsemen in search of manpower, in the last centuries BC, are a possi-bility. Only one fact emerges to bring the prehistory of the Moor to an end: no record exists and no evidence has been found of its occupation during the Roman period (50–400 AD) and the subsequent years of uneasy independence until the coming of the Saxons (650–700 AD). Roman roads found west of Exeter conspicuously avoid the Moor.

Since the Celts survived throughout these centuries—Dr W. G. Hoskins has pointed out the persistence of pre-Saxon physical types in various parts of Devon, including the bor-ders of the Moor—it is also possible that some settlements could have maintained themselves in the Moor valleys. Unfortunately, no settlements, no pottery, no burials (the Celts had re-introduced inhumation), have been found. Continuing occupation even by a few small groups is therefore theory only. After the brief glimpses of Celtic influence on the eastern and western fringes, the picture is a blank for nearly twelve hundred years. The Saxons soon pushed their farms right up to the edge of the Moor, but resettlement of the uplands over 1,000ft does not seem to have taken place at all until the 10th century. It was then that the earliest medieval villages, at such places as Hound Tor and Challacombe, probably originated. The Moor would not have been completely ignored throughout this long period. Hunting and grazing continued, but it seems there was no settlement.

No account of prehistoric Dartmoor is complete without mention of the ponies. They are descended, like all our native breeds, from the small horse brought to Britain by the Celts of Iron Age B. They were trained to draw war-chariots; and Caesar was to pay tribute to the skill of the British charioteers: 'They possess the mobility of cavalry and the steadiness of infantry. By daily practice they are so skilled that they are able to gallop their horses down the steepest ground, to pull up and turn quickly, to run along the pole to the yoke, and then return instantly to the chariot.' In Devon the ability to negotiate steep ground must have been essential. A fine bronze horse-bit, probably attributable to the first century BC, was found in Devon in the 19th–century. Unfortunately, details of the discovery were not recorded, but wherever found, it marks the presence of Celtic horsemen within a day's march of Dartmoor. Bearing in mind also the ring of Iron Age B hill forts surrounding the Moor, it seems reasonable to picture the first ponies running there sometime during the last two centuries BC.

APPENDIX I

ENCLOSED SETTLEMENTS NOT MENTIONED IN THE TEXT

Avon:	Black Tor (3)
	south of Riders Rings (2)
	Bishops Meads
	Huntingdon Warren (3)
	east of Huntingdon Ford
	Hickaton Hill
	Dockwell Ridge (5)
	near Shipley Tor (2)
	Bala Brook (6)
Glazebrook:	Corringdon Ball (2)
	west of Glasscombe corner
	west of Glaze Meet
Erme:	between Hook Lake and Dry Lake (5)
	Harford Moor (2)
	Higher Piles
	east of Addicombe
	Stall Moor (4)
	Tristis Rock
Yealm:	west of Ford Brook (4)
	Pen Beacon (2)

Plym: east of Legis Tor (2)
Lee Moor (4)
Willings Walls Warren
Hentor Brook
Eastern Tor
Shavercombe
Giant's Hill
Drizzlecombe (5)
Lower Hartor

Meavy: south-west slope of Raddick Hill (3)
south-east of Leedon Tor

Walkham: south-west of Leedon Tor
Yellowmeade
Merrivale (2)

East Dart: Lakehead Hill
near Laughter Tor

West Dart: Venford
north of Two Bridges (3)
Cowsic

APPENDIX 2

SOME TYPICAL KISTS NOT MENTIONED IN THE TEXT

Avon:	Brockhill Ford	MR	678657
Erme:	Lower Piles		645603
	Stalldon		632632
	Redlake Foot		637661
Plym:	Willings Walls Warren		584654
	Lee Moor		585644
Meavy:	Down Tor (Narrator Brook)		580692
	Stanlake		564708
Walkham:	Vixen Tor		542744
	Ingra Tor		558721
Lyd:	Doe Tor		544848
Darts:	Hensroost (O Brook)		651707
	near Fox Tor Newtake (Swincombe)		617699
	Fox Tor Newtake (Swincombe)		628713
	Fox Tor Mire (Swincombe)		618704
	Bellever Newtake		641764
	near Cherrybrook		627787
	Stannon Newtake		654811

APPENDIX 3

LOCATION OF FINDS

Exeter Museum:

> Mesolithic flints from Holwell Tor, Postbridge, and
> Taw Marsh
> Wessex arrowhead from Fernworthy
> Finds from Dean Moor enclosed settlement
> Bronze palstave from Horridge Common
> Bronze spearheads from Bloody Pool
> Finds from Kestor Farm

Plymouth Museum:

> Flint Axe from Cosdon Hill
> Stone axehead from near Crockern Tor
> Small kist from Langstone Moor
> Beaker from Chagford Common
> Flints from kist on Lakehead Hill
> Objects from large kist at Merrivale
> Beaker and other finds from cairn at Fernworthy
> Archer's wrist-guard and flint flake from kist near
> Archerton
> Fragments of pottery from kist at Deadman's Bottom
> Arrowheads etc from Northern Dartmoor (Okehampton
> area)

Wessex arrowheads from Grimspound and Postbridge
Pottery and other finds from enclosed settlements at
Legis Tor, Raddick Hill, and Tunhill Rocks; from
villages at Har Tor and Watern Oke; and farms at
White Ridge and Foales Arrishes
Charcoal, burnt bone, and flake from cairn at Stannon
Bottom
Urn from Hurston Ridge
Bronze Rapier from Fice's Well
Bronze ferrule from Gawler Bottom

Torquay Natural History Museum:

Palaeolithic axehead found by R. H. Worth
Mesolithic flints from Gidleigh Common and Runnage
Kist from Thornworthy
Pottery from SmallacombeRocks Farm

Totnes Museum:

Flint knife from Avon valley

BIBLIOGRAPHY

Crossing, William. *Guide to Dartmoor* (David & Charles reprint of 1912 edition). The only full guide to the Moor and still indispensable.

Daniel, Glyn E. *The Prehistoric Chamber-Tombs in England and Wales* (Cambridge 1950). The standard book on megalithic tombs, with references to Corringdon Ball and Cuckoo Ball and the problem of large kists.

Fox, Aileen. *South-West England* (new revised edition David & Charles 1973). The only account of the prehistoric South-west, with many references to Dartmoor.

Worth, R. Hansford. *Dartmoor* (David & Charles reprint 1967). Definitive collection of this great Moorman's writings, including his papers on the prehistoric remains. A mine of information with many photographs, drawings and plans. But Worth died in 1950 and his appraisal of facts was pre-World War II.

Transactions of the Devonshire Association (1862 to date). These contain the reports of the Exploration and Barrow Committees, also full accounts of the modern excavations at Kestor and Dean Moor, the latest information about finds, and lists of sites scheduled as Ancient Monuments.

Reports & Transactions of the Plymouth Institution, Vol 22. 'Some Aspects of a National Park' by H. G. Hurrell: contains a brief account of the excavation of a hut in the Glazebrook valley in 1952.

Articles in the *Proceedings of the Devon Archaeological Society*:

1935   Note on flint knife from Cullever Steps with illustration.

1948   'The Broad Down (Farway) Necropolis and the Wessex Culture in Devon'. Aileen Fox MA FSA.

1953   'A Stone Age settlement system near East Week'. O. Greig and W. M. Rankine.

1968   An article on Bronze Age pottery from Ash Hole, Brixham, by A. M. ApSimon, refers also to pottery styles on Dartmoor.

1969   'Prehistoric and Roman Settlement in Devon and West Somerset'. Aileen Fox MA FSA.

Articles in the *Proceedings of the Prehistoric Society*:

1952   'Prehistoric Settlements on Dartmoor and the Cornish Moors'. C. A. Ralegh Radford. Includes a catalogue of pottery from the Dartmoor settlements with good drawings and photographs; but the conclusions of the article have to be re-assessed in the light of later knowledge.

1954   'Celtic Fields and Farms on Dartmoor'. Lady Aileen Fox. The article which first defined and listed the farm settlements.

1964   'The excavation of a stone alignment and circle at
        Cholwich Town, Lee Moor, Devonshire'. G. Eogan
        and I. G. Simmons.

1969   'Environment and Early Man on Dartmoor'. I. G.
        Simmons. A description of the prehistoric Moor
        based on the results of soil pollen analysis.

        'A Continental Palstave from the Ancient Field Sys-
        tem on Horridge Common, Dartmoor'. Aileen Fox
        and Dennis Britton.

Miscellaneous Accounts:

Antiquity 1938. 'Bronze Age stone monuments on Dartmoor'
    J. W. Brailsford.

Antiquaries Journal Vol 17. A detailed description of the
    Hameldown Dagger by T. A. Kendrick. This is especi-
    ally valuable now that the pommel and blade have been
    destroyed.

Barber, James. Chapter on 'Early Man' in *Dartmoor: A New
    Study* (David & Charles 1970). An excellent up-to-date
    summary.

Fox, Lady Aileen. Chapter on 'Prehistoric Monuments on
    Dartmoor' in the Official Guide to Dartmoor National
    Park (HMSO).

Harvey, L. A. & St Leger Gordon. *Dartmoor* (Collins New
    Naturalists Series 1953), chapter on 'Prehistoric Civilisa-
    tions'.

Hoskins, W. G. *Devon* (Collins 1954). Chapter on 'Prehistoric
    and Celtic Devon'.

INDEX

Page numbers in italics indicate plates

191